TWO FLAGS OVER IWO JIMA

TWO FLAGS OVER IWO JIMA

Solving the Mystery of
the U.S. Marine Corps' Proudest Moment

ERIC HAMMEL

CASEMATE

Philadelphia & Oxford

Published in the United States of America and Great Britain in 2018 by
CASEMATE PUBLISHERS
1950 Lawrence Road, Havertown, PA 19083, USA
and
The Old Music Hall, 106–108 Cowley Road, Oxford OX4 1JE, UK

Hardcover Edition: ISBN 978-1-61200-629-1
Digital Edition: ISBN 978-1-61200-630-7

A CIP record for this book is available from the British Library

Printed and bound in the United States of America

For a complete list of Casemate titles, please contact:

CASEMATE PUBLISHERS (US)
Telephone (610) 853-9131
Fax (610) 853-9146
Email: casemate@casematepublishers.com
www.casematepublishers.com

CASEMATE PUBLISHERS (UK)
Telephone (01865) 241249
Email: casemate-uk@casematepublishers.co.uk
www.casematepublishers.co.uk

This one is for my brother Mark, with love

Til the last landing's made
And we stand unafraid
On a shore no mortal has seen,
Til the last bugle call
Sounds Taps for us all,
It's Semper Fidelis, Marine.

Contents

Author's Note

I would like to start with a little story about me and Joe Rosenthal's immortal "Raising the Flag on Iwo Jima"—The Photo. I have no doubt stories similar to this have been repeated again and again in other places and times over the 75 years since The Photo's first publication.

In 1955 I was a student in Mrs. Lesches's fourth-grade class at Logan Elementary School in Philadelphia. I sat at the last desk in the second row, from which I could look straight out the classroom door to the marble-wainscoted hallway. Opposite the door, and perfectly framed in it from my vantage point, was a large colorized print of The Photo.

I was a good student, and Mrs. Lesches gave me a little slack; I found that I could gaze out the door if she wasn't writing on the blackboard or speaking. So, for the year 1955, I looked out at The Photo every school day, and pretty soon I fell in love with it. I fell in love with my *idea* of it.

I grew up in the company of World War II vets. My own father was one. I knew an Iwo Jima vet. And I was raised in an especially patriotic time and place—post-war America. It stayed with me. In time I found that I could write—indeed, that I wanted to write. In more time I decided to write for my living. In pretty much no time I began to write military history—specifically Pacific War history. And so here I am, 64 years and 50 military history books later, relating a personal story that relates to a photo that relates to that especially poignant and nearly magical long-ago moment on far-off Iwo Jima. The Photo wasn't the only thing that brought me to my vocation, and it wasn't the first. But I have no doubt that that school year of staring at it and imagining heroism crystallized all the other events of my youth that brought me here.

Two Flags over Iwo Jima sets its sights on the 28th Marine Regiment's self-contained battle for Mount Suribachi, the 556-foot-high volcano at Iwo Jima's southwestern peninsula. As the much larger battle for three airfield sites raged to the north, one of eight reinforced Marine regimental combat teams—no more to start with than 4,500 infantrymen and artillerymen supported by a sprinkling of tracked fighting vehicles—undertook the defeat of more than 1,500 heavily armed, highly motivated, and splendidly fortified Japanese combatants who had all pledged to die in order to hold the highest vantage point on the island.

Joe Rosenthal's "Raising the Flag on Iwo Jima" is, bar none, the best-known image of American war history. Most Americans who have no interest in World War II—or *any* war—are nonetheless able to identify the still image of the rough pyramid of "soldiers" with the U.S. flag towering above as "The Flag Raising On Iwo Jima." And many will admit that this 75-year-old image swells their hearts with joy.

Acknowledgements

First and foremost, I could not have begun this book, much less finish it, without the full-bore support of Barbara Hammel, my wife of more than fifty years. Likewise, I'd have been stumped along the way without sage advice from my frend Ted Gradman. Profound thanks to Dick Camp, my pal of more than thirty years, who gave up several days away from his own research to comb archives for material I needed. I also owe a great deal to Walt Ford, the former editor of *Leatherneck* Magazine, for his deep dives into source material and his good advice arising from a complete read of what I had hoped would be the final draft manuscript. I thank Stephen Foley and Dustin Spence for helping me get many photo captions right and for providing several rare photos.

Assisting me all along the way were the kind and helpful folks manning the Marine Corps History Division and the Marine Corps Unversity Archives at Quantico, Virginia. They are Dr. Jim Ginther, Dr. Fred Allison, and Annette Amerman. Questions about the two flags themselves were answered with alacrity by Owen Conner, the heraldry curator at the National Museum of the Marine Corps.

I particularly want to thank Colonel Mary Reinwald, the current editor of *Leatherneck* Magazine and a member of the Huly Board. Mary provided a surge of articles and supporting documents that were vital to my gaining perspective on the story of both flag raisings, from the beginning of my research effort and right up to quite literally the last minute, as I was closing down both the research and writing of this book.

Prologue

It all began at a staff briefing aboard ship on the way from Hawaii to Iwo Jima. A three-dimensional table display of Iwo Jima had been set up to provide officers of the 5th Marine Division's 2nd Battalion, 28th Marine Regiment (28th Marines) with a realistic view of their battalion's and regiment's area of responsibility in the early phases of the invasion.[1]

Colonel Harry Liversedge's reinforced 28th Marines had been given a mission quite different from the other five regimental combat teams assigned to the 4th and 5th Marine divisions. While the rest of Major General Harry Schmidt's V Amphibious Corps (VAC) attacked northward to secure Iwo Jima's three airfields, Liversedge's force was to attack independently to the south in order to defang and put to use the excellent vantage point afforded by the 556-foot-high Suribachi volcano (also known as Hill 556 after its height in feet).

As the staff and senior officers of the 2nd Battalion, 28th Marines studied the mock-up of the island, someone commented on the steep, rough terrain represented by the volcano, adding that the first Marines to get to the summit would deserve a prize. Someone else quipped, "Champagne." At which Captain Dave Severance, Company E's veteran 25-year-old commander, thought to himself that they wouldn't need much champagne because not too many people were going to get up the rugged, well-defended mountain.[2]

The battalion adjutant, Second Lieutenant George Greeley Wells, then spoke up to mention that the current Marine Corps staff manual required that all battalion adjutants carry the United States colors on all operations. Wells added that he had a flag in his possession—provided by the battalion's transport, USS *Missoula*—and that he would provide it, when the moment came, to the first Marines dispatched to climb to the volcano's summit.[3]

This brief exchange had the most profound effect on Lieutenant Colonel Chandler Johnson, the 2nd Battalion commanding officer.

It was thus that the United States Marine Corps' proudest moment was built on one man's wish. An infantry battalion commander wished his unit had a history-making memento of the battle it would be fighting. Toward that end, he dispatched a reconnaissance party composed of 45 of his Marines up a volcano his regiment had besieged but was not quite ready to definitively attack. He also dispatched an American flag that he wanted back as a memento for his battalion; if all went well, it would be the first American flag to fly over core Imperial Japanese territory. A Marine photographer joined the reconnaissance party and climbed the mountain while taking photos, then took photos of the United States national colors that had been raised at the summit.

Event piled on event until a civilian photographer, another Marine photographer, and a Marine movie cameraman arrived, as did a second flag. By then, the battalion commander wanted the first flag—what he thought of as his unit's flag—brought safely to his hands. The much larger second flag was a good substitute that could be seen from almost any point on the embattled island. As long as it flew, it provided a bracing morale boost for Marines locked in a death grip with their Japanese adversaries.

This is how History is made.

Maps

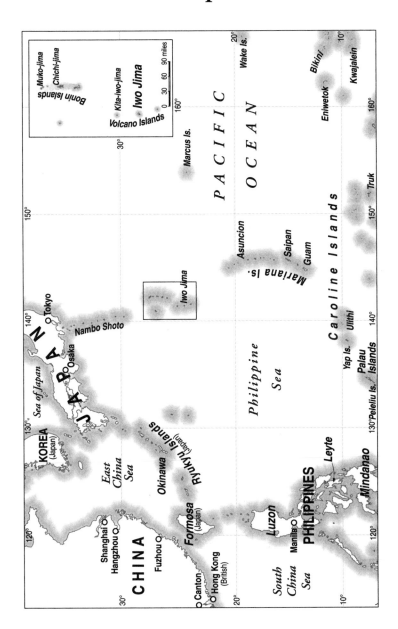

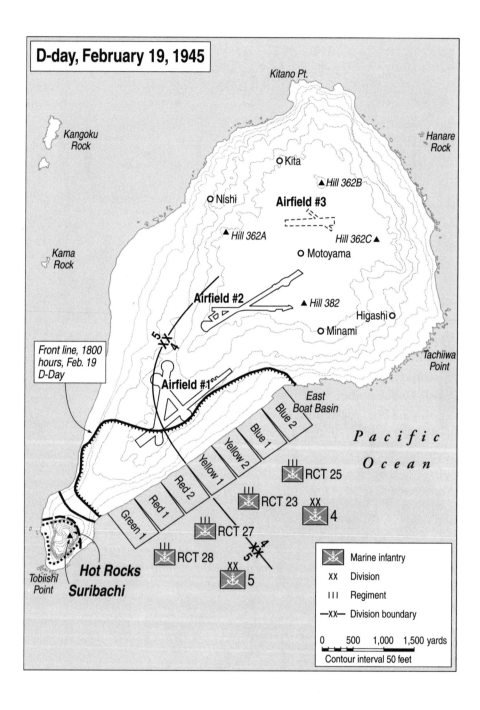

D-day, February 19, 1945

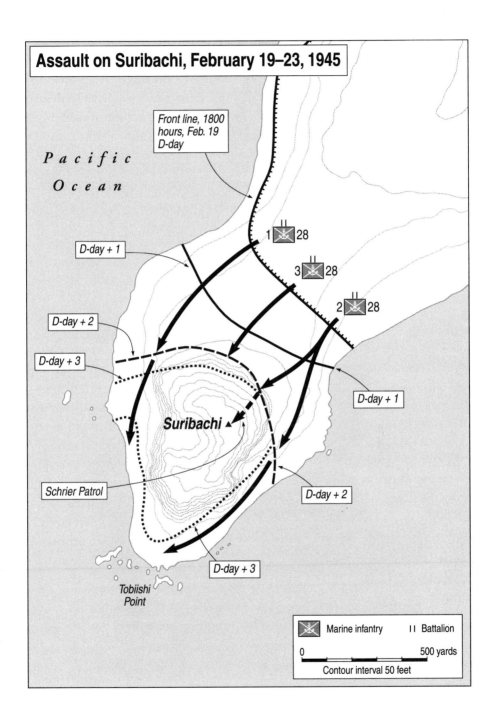

Assault on Suribachi, February 19–23, 1945

Pacific
Ocean

Front line, 1800 hours, Feb. 19 D-day

1 28

3 28

2 28

D-day + 1

D-day + 2

D-day + 3

D-day + 1

Suribachi

Schrier Patrol

D-day + 2

D-day + 3

Tobiishi Point

Marine infantry   ǁ Battalion

0   500 yards

Contour interval 50 feet

CHAPTER I

Before

Why Iwo Jima?

Iwo Jima is one of the most isolated places on Earth. Waterless and barren, it is unsubtly hostile to human settlement. Today, fewer than 400 people inhabit the island—all members of the Japan Self-Defense Force. The island is open to international travelers just one day a year—around the February 19 anniversary of the invasion—and only American and Japanese pilgrims, historians, and history buffs make the journey.

Today, as in days predating the opening of Japan to the world in the mid-19th century, Iwo Jima rests at the very outer limit of the empire. Her only economic function has been the export of sulfur, a byproduct of the volcanic action that seethes barely beneath the island's mantle.

During the first four years of the Pacific War, Iwo Jima had only two functions: as a watch post against invasion of the inner empire, and as the seat of an air base complex built to enhance her garrison's watch mission. But her importance to Japan in late 1944 and early 1945 was also emotional; Iwo Jima, nearly useless though it was, was nonetheless an integral component of the empire. Also, because she could support several large airfields—which nearby islands could not—she would naturally come under the eye of the American naval, air, and amphibious forces sweeping across the vast Pacific toward the Japanese home islands. The reasons for stoutly defending the otherwise useless and barren volcanic speck was first one of honor—for Iwo Jima was intrinsically Japanese; second, to deny the Americans the airfield sites for as long as possible; and third, to lay down the gauntlet, to communicate to the onrushing Americans that all of Japan would be as stoutly, as heroically, as unremittingly defended as was tiny, useless—but oh so Japanese—Iwo.

The bloodbath at Iwo Jima in late February and most of March 1945 owes itself entirely to the exigencies of the air war in the Pacific as a whole and specifically to the needs of the culminating phase of the strategic air offensive against the Japanese home islands.

Until mid-1944, when U.S. Marine and Army divisions seized Japanese-held Saipan, Tinian, and Guam in the Mariana Islands, the Allied Pacific War strategy had been hobbled by the operational range (i.e. the effective combat radius) of land-based fighters. Simply put, to run an effective land-based bombing campaign against Japanese-held Pacific island bases, the U.S. Army Air Forces, Navy, and Marine air commands in the Pacific had to provide numerous and effective fighter escorts. So, though bombers outranged fighters by a considerable margin, the advance up the Solomons chain in 1942 and 1943, along the northern coast of New Guinea from late 1942 to mid-1944, across the central Pacific in late 1943 through mid-1944, and through the Philippines from September 1944 had to take place at a pace of up to 300 miles per hop if the objective was to seize airfield sites from which Japanese bases farther out could be effectively interdicted by fighter-escorted, land-based bombers.

This linkage between the Allied Pacific offensive and the operational range of fighters (which was less than half their actual range) held up as a military law of nature until the unveiling of the U.S. Navy's fast carrier task force in late 1943. At that point, as new fleet carriers and light carriers began to arrive in the Pacific war zone at an average rate in excess of one per month, the 300-mile law could be bent somewhat if enough carriers could be shackled to a new objective long enough for ground troops to either seize an existing airfield that could be *quickly* rehabilitated or clear room for the *rapid* installation of a new airfield. As land-based fighters, fighter-bombers, and single-engine light bombers moved up to the new airfield, land-based, multi-engine medium and heavy bombers also could be brought forward, to support invasion troops ashore as well as to strike nearby bases that had been kept under the gun to that point by carrier air strikes. At that juncture, the full weight of the fast carrier task force could be used to soften up new targets beyond the operational range of land-based fighters and, as the central Pacific campaign progressed, even beyond the effective range of land-based bombers. The addition of numerous escort carriers to the invasion fleets from late 1943 substantially enhanced the reach of the fast carriers, because escort-based air squadrons were trained and equipped to guard the invasion fleet *and* provide air support for forces ashore. Thus more fast carriers could move on to more distant assignments sooner than had been the case prior to the organization of flotillas of escort carriers.

The technological leap that nearly severed the link between the length of a new step forward and the operational range of land-based fighters was the appearance of U.S. Army Air Forces Boeing B-29 Superfortress very heavy bombers. These aerial leviathans, which were first employed out of forward bases in China, were built to fly at 32,000 feet—higher than most Japanese defensive fighters could reach—as well as to carry four tons of bombs out to ranges of 1,600 miles, and return. This was about 5,000 feet higher and 600 miles farther *in each direction* than the tried-and-true Consolidated B-24 Liberator heavy bomber.

The seizure of Saipan, Tinian, and Guam would place nearly all of Japan within range of a B-29-based bombing offensive as soon as highly reinforced, extra-long runways could be built on the three islands.

The first B-29s reached Saipan on October 12, 1944; several groups ran a training mission against Japanese-held-but-bypassed Truk on October 28; and six of 17 B-29s dispatched from Guam attacked Iwo Jima on November 8 (at a range of nearly 650 miles), the first of several winter "training" missions to Iwo. Finally, on the night of February 4, 1945, 69 Marianas-based XXI Bomber Command B-29s flew all the way to Kobe, while 30 other B-29s that failed to find the city bombed targets of opportunity and of last resort. Two B-29s failed to return.[1]

Other than as a practice target in the run-up to the February 4 attack, Iwo Jima as yet had no direct role in the B-29 strategy, but the island stood at the apex of a shallow equilateral triangle, roughly half the distance between the Marianas and central Japan.

By early 1945, all three of the Army Air Forces' long-range, high-altitude fighter types of the day—Lockheed P-38 Lightnings, Consolidated P-47 Thunderbolts, and North American P-51 Mustangs—had been refined to the point at which their operational range was more than the distance between Iwo Jima and Tokyo. In other words, Iwo Jima, as an air base, stood at an optimum point for emergency landings by damaged or malfunctioning B-29s on their way to or from Japan and the Marianas—*and* as the extreme launch point for long-range fighters that could provide daylight escort for B-29s over Japanese cities and industrial zones.[2]

In a nutshell, Iwo Jima or a neighboring island in the Volcano or Bonin island groups were the most suitable sites for an emergency airfield and advance escort-fighter base in support of the upcoming strategic bombing offensive against the Japanese homeland. All of the calculus by which invasion targets were selected that late in the Pacific War ground out inexorable results to all of the mathematical inputs bound up in distances and even in the tradeoffs in lives laid on the line to seize the bases as opposed to lives saved by having airfields available for emergency landings, not to mention fighter escorts that could reach central Japan. Indeed, twin-engine North American B-25 medium bombers (designated PBJ by the Marine Corps) would be able to attack Japanese shipping and shore targets in southern Japan from Iwo Jima, a minor but nonetheless interesting bonus.[3]

There were other islands in the vicinity of Iwo Jima that would have been fine as advance support bases that late in the war, but Iwo Jima was the only one whose topography could support the very long runways required by the B-29s. The Japanese did not realize this, because they knew very little about the B-29 program. Nevertheless, they very well comprehended the offensive value Iwo Jima would have if the largest, longest-ranged American heavy bomber of the last phase of the Pacific War would have remained the B-24, because B-24s based at or staging through Iwo Jima from the Marianas would nonetheless have complete access to all of Japan. Moreover, they knew that Iwo-based, state-of-the-art fighter escorts would be able to range over all of the southern two-thirds of Japan.

Even without factoring in the B-29 program, the Japanese knew that Iwo Jima was a highly likely target for American strategic planners, so they decided to defend it as heavily as their reeling war industry and burgeoning manpower needs (and declining manpower) could support. The fact that Iwo Jima stood at the extremity of the pre-war Japanese Empire added honor—and thus intractable stubbornness, or even fanaticism—to the mix of defensive priorities in a way American invasion forces had not yet experienced in the Pacific.[4]

Fortress Iwo

The Japanese architect of the Iwo Jima battle plan was Lieutenant General Tadamichi Kuribayashi, who was handed his assignment to defend the volcanic island directly by the prime minister, General Hideki Tojo, in late May 1944—a month ahead of the first American carrier strikes. Even then the Japanese strategists knew that their defense of Iwo would be a rearguard battle fought to gain time for the bitter defense of the home islands to take shape.

Kuribayashi was a well-traveled 54-year-old who had served two of his 30 years in uniform in the United States. He knew what he was up against in terms of industrial might and described Americans thusly: "[T]he people are energetic and versatile. One must never underestimate the American's fighting ability."[5]

The new island commander, who reached Iwo during the second week of June 1944, experienced American energy once again through all of the summer's air attacks, during which the island's air-defense contingent was virtually annihilated. Certain the attacks presaged an imminent direct invasion, Kuribayashi and the rest of the island's too-few defenders awaited a similar annihilation. They were flabbergasted when it failed to materialize.

As Kuribayashi settled in to his apparently final service to his emperor, his thinking departed radically from—but built upon—that of colleagues all across the wide Pacific. Rather than bank everything on an all-out beachside defense that offered little to no defensive depth, Kuribayashi ordered his troops to construct interlocking defenses throughout the island's rough interior. And rather than hold troops back to participate in a desperate, all-out mass counterattack—a so-called *banzai*—in the open, he decreed that nearly every defender must remain in place, under good cover, until blown up or pried out on the point of a bayonet. And the entire island would be covered beneath interlocking fans of artillery, mortars, and rockets. The Japanese defensive tactics American planners had come to rely upon for quick victory on Pacific islands would not be used; Kuribayashi's brief to gain time for the homeland defense dictated a long, bloody battle of attrition.

As the troops already on Iwo dug in, Kuribayashi's nominal and newly activated 109th Infantry Division began to be filled out with reinforcements. The 5,000-man 2d Independent Mixed Brigade was transferred from Chichi Jima, and the 2,700-man 15th Infantry Regiment, which had been earmarked for Saipan before that island was invaded in June 1944, also was sent to Iwo. Next to arrive was a 1,200-man naval construction battalion, followed by 2,200 elite naval infantry troops and sufficient aviation ground personnel. A mixed bag of artillery units and five antitank battalions came next, but thereafter U.S. Navy submarines clung to the sea lanes to Iwo, sinking many supply ships through the late summer and autumn. One spread of torpedoes took to the bottom most of the barbed wire to be allotted to Iwo, and all 28 of the vehicles of the tank regiment assigned to Iwo also were lost with their transport. Nevertheless, 22 tanks were replaced in due course (every one of them was dug in to a static emplacement) and the artillery strength rose to 361 artillery pieces rated at 75mm or over, 94 dual-purpose antiaircraft guns rated 75mm or over, 33 dual-purpose naval guns rated 80mm or over, 12 320mm spigot mortars, 65 150mm and 81mm mortars, more than 200 20mm and 25mm antiaircraft guns, 69 47mm and 37mm antitank guns, and an array of 70 rocket weapons with warheads rated between 200 pounds and 550 pounds. Lighter weapons included every type offered to ground-combat units of the Imperial Army and Imperial Navy, from infantry rifles and light, medium, and heavy machine guns to the small 70mm field guns assigned to infantry battalions. There were gaps in weapons rations caused by American action against the sea lanes, but, one way or another, every defensive unit achieved more or less its assigned fighting capability.[6]

Fully 25 percent of the troops who reached Iwo were assigned to tunneling operations. The tunnels were designed for two purposes: deep protection against air attack and interior lines of communication that would be maximally difficult for invaders to sever. Every type of defensive emplacement or bunker imaginable was built, from one-man spider holes to huge underground living and command bunkers. Many individual and crewed light-weapon emplacements were lined with stone or even constructed from precast concrete.[7]

In the end, even though General Kuribayashi's defensive arrangements were not completed, Iwo Jima was in a class by itself, the ultimate expression of death and mayhem for the sake of death and mayhem to be found in the annals of the Pacific War. Improving exponentially on a "defend and die" concept first encountered by U.S. Army troops on Biak, an island off New Guinea, and then by Marines at Peleliu, the island commander insisted upon the construction of hundreds of bunkers, pillboxes, blockhouses, and other fighting positions as well as multistory underground command centers and underground barracks—some as deep at 75 feet, and all interconnected by D-day by eleven miles of underground passageways.

Reinforcements continued to arrive until early February 1945. Thus an estimated 23,000 Imperial troops, many of them veterans, were on hand to defend Iwo. The hundreds of mortars, artillery pieces, and rockets emplaced throughout the internal defensive sectors were painstakingly preregistered to cover virtually every square yard of the island. Nearly all the defenders had been bonded into a brotherhood born of rugged training (70 percent of their waking time) and the extreme difficulties encountered during the building of bunkers and passageways underground in extreme heat laced with sulfurous fumes. Beyond that, all the defenders took a solemn oath to fight to the death, to give no ground for any reason short of death. All questions of counterattacking the invaders were quelled when Kuribayashi sacked 18 senior officers who openly disagreed with his static-defense strategy; except for designated roving assault detachments, the defenders would man their positions unto death. Indeed, each and every Japanese on the island took a solemn oath to the Emperor to fight to the death, and to kill ten Americans before he died.[8]

CHAPTER 2

Invasion

Company E

This is Company E—about 250 Marines and hospital corpsmen strong. Forty percent of the Marines in the company are former Marine Raiders or paramarines; the other 60 percent are well schooled in the art of war but not yet personally familiar with it.[1] Together with Company D and Company F, Company E forms the infantry component of the 2nd Battalion, 28th Marine Regiment. Company E, as were all U.S. Marine companies since mid-1944, is composed of three 45-man rifle platoons (numbered 1st, 2nd, and 3rd), plus a small headquarters component, a machine-gun section, and a 60mm mortar section. Each rifle platoon is composed of three rifle squads of about ten men each plus a ten- or eleven-man assault squad manned by flamethrower operators, bazooka teams, and demolitions assault men.[2] Each rifle squad is composed of three three-man fire teams (team leader, rifleman, automatic rifleman) plus the squad leader. The infantry squads are usually employed to engage and pin down enemy soldiers manning fixed defensive positions while the flamethrower operators, bazooka teams, and demolitions assault men burn out and/or blow up the enemy's fixed defensive positions. Being a member of a Marine rifle platoon in early 1945 requires bravery, skill, and a notion of teamwork and shared responsibility. Being unskilled or too deliberative or irresponsible to squad mates and fire-team mates could easily point the way to an early grave for all concerned.

A small minority of the men of Company E will be the main focus of the action in this story. Here is an introduction to one of them, as he was on the way to Beach Green, the southernmost landing beach on Iwo Jima, on D-day morning, February 19, 1945.

Severance

Dave E. Severance, the commanding officer of Company E, 2nd Battalion, 28th Marines, was born in Milwaukee on July 4, 1919, and grew up in Colorado. He left home to attend college in Seattle in 1936, but quit after a year to earn tuition money. He enlisted in the Marine Corps because he was told he would be taught how to fly. At boot camp in San Diego, he was told he would not be allowed to fly, so he went to sea for several years and was promoted corporal, a rank he had held earlier as an underage member of the Colorado National Guard. Corporal Severance, an imposing 6 feet, 2 inches tall, volunteered for parachute training in July 1941 even though most paramarines were rather slight of build. He prospered, was promoted sergeant in April 1942, and subsequently offered a commission as a second lieutenant when he was scheduled to be shipped to the Pacific war zone. Lieutenant Severance commanded a paramarine platoon on Bougainville, in the northern Solomon Islands, in late 1943 and saw his first action in that capacity. When the paramarine regiment was disbanded in February 1944, Severance was posted to the new 5th Marine Division, which was being stood up at Camp Pendleton, California. He was ordered to join the 28th Marines as soon as he reported in following home leave.[3] At the regimental command post, the new captain was offered an assignment to the battalion of his choice, so he asked who the battalion commanders were. He knew two of the men named and decided not to risk working for either of them, so he opted for the man about whom he knew nothing, the 2nd Battalion's Lieutenant Colonel Chandler Johnson.[4]

"Johnson was sort of a maverick," Severance noted in a 2008 interview, "I don't know all the details, but he was a feisty, heavyset guy. He was fat and fearless. He had a sense of humor and he had a rage about him, and he had a thin line between the two. You never knew which way he was going. But I liked him. I liked him a lot."[5]

Johnson

Chandler Wilce Johnson was born in Fort Dodge, Iowa, on October 8, 1905, and entered the United States Naval Academy at Annapolis from Illinois as a member of the Class of 1929. He thereafter spent a lot of time overseas, serving as an infantry officer in Nicaragua, the Philippines, and Hawaii as well as postings in the United States. During the first week of June 1942, he first saw combat as the major commanding the 3rd Defense Battalion's 3-inch Antiaircraft Gun Group in

Midway Atoll as a reinforcement to the 6th Defense Battalion. Johnson subsequently commanded his gun group during the whole of the six-month Guadalcanal campaign and beyond. On June 1, 1943, he was given medical orders to return to the United States for treatment of malaria. In mid-July he was ordered to Camp Lejeune, North Carolina, then to attend the U.S. Army's Command and General Staff School at Fort Leavenworth, Kansas. He was awarded the Legion of Merit in October 1943 for his service at Guadalcanal.[6]

D-day

On February 19, 1945, following an intense 74-day air and naval bombardment, two veteran regiments of the 4th Marine Division landed alongside two green regiments of the new 5th Marine Division on the black sand-and-ash beaches of southern Iwo Jima. As warships and warplanes pummeled targets all across the island, the first wave of troop-filled amphibian tractors (amtracs) climbed ashore.

Nothing happened. There was no return fire. No Japanese fired at the ships offshore, nor at the oncoming waves of amtracs, nor at Marines who were surprised to learn this as their feet sought purchase in the soft, shifting black ground. Wave upon wave landed on eerily peaceful beaches. The largest force of U.S. Marines ever assembled had come to fight for Iwo Jima, and it appeared to be getting a free pass.

It's possible that some of the rigorously trained Americans—possibly a minority—would have preferred to have had to kick the door open with guns ablazing, something more in keeping with the spirit of hours and days and weeks of rigorous training followed by days and weeks and months of rigorous waiting. Something to take the edge off? But they were all dealt the same hand: more waiting for the known twenty-plus thousands of Japanese on Iwo Jima to turn on the heat. Meantime, it was lay low and reorganize under this unexpected dispensation.

The descent to hell began as the lead units advanced up the bluff commanding the beach. The world fell in on them as pre-registered mortar fire erupted on and around every living man. The Marines had walked into and laid down on the kill zone.

There was mayhem at the beach. Infantry could manage after a fashion; there was always a way to get forward on foot, but anything with wheels sank to its axles, and even the treads on tanks and amtracs slipped and dug into the bottomless ash. As the day progressed, a high inshore tidal surge forced scores of landing craft to broach in the surf.

At the front, the infantrymen quickly adapted. Unable to dig in, they attacked every fighting position they could see and reach, and then they went looking for more. The reserve battalions were landed and thrown into the fight at the front or cleared bypassed positions behind the front. In due course, tanks and heavy weapons found their way to the front. But it was the brave infantrymen who took the ground from other brave infantrymen, all of them heedless of their lives.

Company E on D-day

Company E was the 28th Marines regimental reserve, to be used to plug holes in the regimental line, to stem a counterattack, or to undertake any other mission to which the regimental commander saw a need to commit it. The company headquarters, two rifle platoons, and most of the company's crew-served weapons made the trip from transport to the extreme left (southern) flank of Beach Green in crowded amphibian tractors assigned to the tenth landing wave. Roughly 40 minutes after the first Americans hit Beach Green, the landing beach nearest to the Suribachi volcano, the main body of Company E began its final approach.

By the time the tenth wave was in range of Japanese mortars, many of those weapons were in resolute action against the Marine battalion landing teams stalled on or still approaching the beaches from the south. The amtracs bearing Company E were passing beneath 556-foot-high Mount Suribachi and still several hundred yards from the beach when Corporal Robert Leader, a member of the 3rd Platoon's 2nd Squad, was able to hear the pinging sound of machine gun bullets striking the shield of the starboard heavy machine gun he was manning. The bullets went on to pass close over the head of an amtrac crewmen.[7]

Nearly as soon as Company E's amtracs began to disgorge their passengers, seven of Captain Dave Severance's Marines had been wounded by the mortars. An eighth nearly drowned when he leaped from the amtrac's rear ramp while loaded down with rifle, pack, a can of belted machine-gun bullets, and a satchel filled with explosives. At first, no one appeared to notice this man's plight, but someone bumped into him and realized that he was stuck underwater, held down by his heavy load. The nearly drowned Marine was assisted to the beach and turned in at a beachside aid station.[8]

Bradley

John Henry Bradley was born in Antigo, Wisconsin, on July 10, 1923, and grew up in Appleton. He graduated from high school in 1941 and proceeded to fulfill his ambition of becoming a funeral worker by completing an 18-month course under a local funeral director. He enlisted in the U.S. Navy on January 13, 1943, in response to his father's advice that he avoid ground combat. On completion of boot camp in Bayview, Idaho, Bradley was assigned in March 1943 to the Navy Hospital Corps School, Farragut, Idaho, and upon graduation began a tour at the naval hospital in Oakland, California. In January 1944, he was reassigned to the Fleet Marine Force and trained for ground combat at a field medical school in San Diego. Then it was off to the 5th Marine Division and duty with Company E, 2nd Battalion, 28th Marines on April 15, 1944.[9]

Pharmacist's Mate Second Class John Bradley was caught up in casualty treatment duty from the moment he reached Iwo Jima's southernmost landing beach—Beach Green. The first man in Company E's 3rd Platoon to be wounded was the 1st Squad's Private First Class John Fredotovich, an automatic rifleman. He and the rest of the 3rd Platoon had occupied a position from which they could bolster the 1st Battalion's drive across the island to seal off Suribachi and its potent garrison. The platoon was in stasis and under limited cover when 18-year-old Fredotovich heard a mortar round detonate very close by. Before he had time to register another thought, he felt a cold chill pass over his body as shrapnel embedded itself in his right side, where it carved one wound from his buttocks to his knee and a large shard caved in his ribs from beneath his armpit to his shoulder blade. Shrapnel in his thigh broke his femur. On Fredotovich's left side, where he was shielded from the spray of shrapnel, the youngster's fire-team leader, Corporal Richard Wheeler, rose to his knees, bellowed for assistance from a corpsman, and administered sulfa tablets with sips of water.[10]

Doc Bradley, who had ridden ashore in the same amtrac as Fredotovich, kneeled beside the stocky Marine while forcefully waving away a knot of rubberneckers and shouting, "Leave the man alone; he's badly hurt."[11] As the wounded man's overloaded circuits carried his mind in and out of consciousness, Bradley proceeded to fight the potentially fatal shock with blood transfusions. As soon as Fredotovich was stable enough, Bradley organized four onlookers to carry him to the spot on the beach set aside for casualties designated for treatment aboard a ship equipped to provide hospital-like capabilities.[12]

Thurman Fogarty, another young Marine on his first day of battle, was scraping out a little indentation just above the surf line when he felt someone beside him. He looked up to see that John Bradley was treating a small wound in his own leg. As Fogarty continued to scrape out some protection from the storm of steel and lead, he spotted another Marine to his left whose arm was all but shredded from his shoulder. When he pointed out the man with the terrible arm wound to Bradley, the corpsman immediately rolled over Fogarty to begin treating the wound. First off, Bradley applied a tourniquet to the bloody stump and explained its use before turning it over to the control of the wounded man. Next, Bradley anesthetized the pain with morphine before lashing the wounded arm to the stump. And then he pointed toward the beach-side evacuation site and told the casualty to walk there under his own power. Throughout the time he was treating an endless stream of casualties, Bradley and his casualties were vulnerable to unceasing mortar, artillery, and small-arms fire. In addition to his own urgent work ministering to the wounded, Doc Bradley, as senior company corpsman, had to manage the six docs under his authority, including assigning out his corpsmen to adjacent and intermingled units whose own corpsmen had been killed or wounded. There is no telling how many lives John Bradley saved through direct action or good management throughout D-day of the precious asset of medical expertise.[13]

Severance

As soon as he stepped ashore, Company E's Captain Dave Severance turned in the direction of a network of tank traps—wide, deep trenches meant to stall tanks arriving ashore and deploying to attack Japanese strongpoints. The tank traps marked the Company E assembly area.

The bulk of Company E arrived and went to work reorganizing for any eventuality, but Second Lieutenant Ed Pennell's 2nd Platoon, which was carried to Iwo Jima aboard landing craft rather than amphibian tractors, was nowhere to be found. This was just dawning on Severance when he was summoned to meet with the regimental commander at the latter's command post, which was 30 yards away.

Colonel Harry Liversedge was a big man: at least 6-4 to Severance's 6-2. Known as "Harry the Horse," he was a storied athlete in Marine Corps circles, having won a bronze medal for shot put in the 1920 Olympics. He had participated in the 1924 Olympics as well. More recently, he had commanded the 1st Marine Raider Regiment in action in the central Solomon Islands in mid-1943 and had stood up the 28th Marines.

When Dave Severance arrived at the regimental command post, the colonel noted that Japanese to the north appeared to be preparing a counterattack against the regimental beachhead area, and asked if Company E was ready to repel boarders. To which the company commander acceded that his 2nd Platoon had not yet turned up from wherever it had landed—*if* it had landed.

The harried colonel leveled a finger at the captain: "I'll give you five minutes to get the platoon in here or I'm going to give you a general court martial." Duly noted. Severance started back to the company assembly area.

First thing, Severance used a walkie-talkie to try to raise the errant platoon. No go; the frequency was oversubscribed by at least a double handful of Marines trying to reach other Marines.

Well trained to study options on the fly and settle on a solution, Severance considered the possibilities: the platoon had been sunk before it reached the beach; or it was lost in the chaos ashore; or it had not received a message that the company assembly area had been moved. The options for action were stark: lie to the colonel and claim the platoon had arrived—if the Japanese attacked, two platoons and machine guns and light mortars would likely be enough to stop them—or admit failure.

As the captain neared the assembly area and juggled the options, he ran into Captain Fred Haynes, the 28th Marines assistant operations officer, who stopped him to talk. Everything was okay: Second Lieutenant Ed Pennell's 2nd Platoon was farther inland than it was supposed to be and was awaiting orders. As soon as Severance ordered Pennell to join the company's main body, the 2nd Platoon broke cover to hike south along the fire-swept beach.

Sergeant Michael Strank, whom Captain Severance considered Company E's best, most admirable noncommissioned officer, took it on himself to teach the young tyros in his care about grace under fire. As the company slunk southward in awkward poses of fear, Strank sat down and, with his spine conspicuously straight, methodically removed his boondockers—Marine Corps combat boots—and socks and shook out the embedded sand. Then he methodically reshod his feet and rose to lope along the beach in a mode that can only be described as relaxed. Farther along, as the youngsters were exposed to the sounds of explosions and gunfire they became less and less rattled. Sergeant Strank stalked backward and forward among his charges, cautioning them to maintain prudent intervals and "Don't bunch up!"[14] Ever so slowly, the overwhelming, mind-numbing general cacophony of war was transformed by such lessons and advice into background noise.

Late on D-day afternoon, Sergeant Mike Strank's assistant squad leader, Corporal Harlon Block, was leading a line of crawling 2nd Platoon Marines along a fire-swept trench when he suddenly stopped and was head-butted by the next man in line, whose helmet restricted the view ahead. When he looked to see what was going on, the Marine behind Block saw that Block was fixated on a pair of legs attached to hips that were cut off from an unseen torso. As the truth seeped along the line of 2nd Platoon men, Corporal Block suggested softly, "Why don't we bury him."

Also that afternoon, the publicly upbeat Sergeant Mike Strank confided in a friend, "This is my third campaign, and I'm not going to make it through this one."

The anticipated Japanese attack never materialized. As the 1st Battalion, 28th Marines, advanced to cut Mount Suribachi off from the rest of Iwo Jima's defenders, the 2nd Battalion stood in reserve to guard the regimental beachhead until it was sent forward in the afternoon to take down several bypassed defensive structures.[15]

Following in the trace of the 1st Battalion, Company E hiked a long distance in a single file that telescoped in and out as the undiminished Japanese artillery, mortars, machine guns, and rifles kept it pretty much constantly under fire. One shell burst completely buried the 3rd Platoon's Corporal Robert Leader beneath a load of sand and volcanic ash, squeezing him so tightly that he could not dig his way out. As Leader's air supply dwindled, his fire team turned to and saved him.

Private Leo Rozek, a 3rd Platoon rifleman, was one of a number of Marines who scraped a shallow hole for himself whenever and wherever there was a halt in the platoon's progress. At one stop, he was stunned to find that his digging unearthed a Japanese mine, an incident that repeated itself shortly after he moved to dig another hole.

During one long break, Corporal Dick Wheeler found time to engage Corporal Charles Lindberg in conversation. Wheeler had enlisted earlier in the war than most, but he had missed combat for nearly the entire war due to a non-combat assignment. Chuck Lindberg was also an early enlistee who had joined the Marine Raiders, with which he first faced combat on Guadalcanal and graduated to several other combat operations before being assigned to Company E and volunteering to become a flamethrower operator. At length, Wheeler uttered, "Well, it looks as though I finally rate my battle star." To which Lindberg responded, "You'd better wait and see if you get off this rock in one piece." And then Lindberg climbed to the top of the terrace that was shielding the 3rd Platoon. In the space of one quick peek at the terrain ahead, a mortar round detonated virtually in his face. Addled by the unexpected blast, Lindberg required a few moments to determine that he had shed no blood but that a small piece of shrapnel had dented his helmet. He turned to Dick Wheeler while fingering the dent in his helmet and said, "See what I mean?"[16]

Before the breather was called, two large landing ships beached adjacent to the terrace the 3rd Platoon had occupied. They drew immediate shell fire as their ramps were deployed. The leader of the 3rd Platoon, Lieutenant John "Keith" Wells—known as Jenghis Khan, a play on his own initials and a commentary on his aggressive nature—happened to be standing tall as the first heavy rounds detonated, and showed no inclination to get down behind the terrace. Without a by-your-leave, one of the enlisted combat veterans rose beside Wells and simply knocked him off his feet. On the way down, the officer felt a load of shrapnel pass through just where he was standing.[17]

Soon, orders arrived for Company E (still the regimental reserve) to move closer to the front lines: Captain Severance and most of Company E awaited the 2nd Platoon's arrival at the company rendezvous.[18]

Desperate Combat

Meanwhile, at Iwo Jima's narrowest point, two companies of the 1st Battalion, 28th Marines—Captain Phil Roach's Company C and Captain Dwayne "Bobo" Mears's Company B—drove to the western shore with a costly gallantry. Both company commanders led small teams of volunteers at the heads of their units, knocking out position after position. After attacking numerous pillboxes and bunkers while armed with only a.45-caliber automatic pistol, Mears was belatedly evacuated and eventually hospitalized from the effects of his (mortal) neck wound, which also severed most of his tongue. Roach, who constantly exposed himself to Japanese fire as he directed his troops, was incapacitated by merely "serious" wounds. In the wake of conspicuous leaders like these, Marines who lost track of their own units were inspired to join forces with other stragglers to take out mutually supporting fighting positions whose interlocking fields of fire swept over all Marines, lost and found, all along and behind the front. Marine mortars with no cover and just the rounds that could be carried to them were fired directly at targets that their crews could see with their own eyes, a situation rare on modern battlefields.

By late morning, ten Marines from two platoons of Bobo Mears's Company B joined forces on the 1st Battalion's objective, the western beach at Iwo Jima's narrowest point, 700 yards from Beach Green. Behind these brave but exhausted Marines, the 2nd Battalion, 28th Marines, (less Company E) mopped up and established a continuous line across the island's narrow neck, then faced the southwestern tail of the island, which was dominated by the island's signature terrain feature: forbidding Mount Suribachi. Specifically, companies D and F were sent to the left to clear the approaches to the northern and western base of the volcano while, in its first real offensive move of the day, Company E was halfway released from the regimental reserve to achieve and maintain firm physical contact with the 1st Battalion and string itself backward to secure the supply route from Beach Green and the 28th Marines' burgeoning logistics base as well as to sanitize bypassed Japanese bunkers, pillboxes, and caves.

Until late on D-day morning, the 3rd Battalion, 28th Marines, was held as the V Amphibious Corps floating reserve, but Colonel Harry Liversedge petitioned the 5th Marine Division commanding general for release of the fresh battalion to go to the aid of the vastly diminished and disorganized 1st Battalion in holding a safe margin of maneuver room against possible counterattacks. As the first elements of the 3rd Battalion came ashore shortly after noon, they were pounded by mortars and artillery that inflicted numerous casualties and damage to equipment. Follow-on elements of the battalion landing team were similarly savaged. The notion that the shocked and bleeding 3rd Battalion could move up behind the wrecked 1st Battalion in order that both could reach and spread around the foot of the volcano simply wasn't going to happen on February 19; both battalions needed to collect their wits and reorganize. That left two 2nd Battalion companies—D and F—available to Lieutenant Colonel Chandler Johnson to do the work of two battalions. What Colonel Liversedge got for his having had his truncated 2nd Battalion move to contact with the Japanese was two desultory late-afternoon company-size attacks against the powerful garrison established in uncountable hidden emplacements on and around the volcano. (Rather than leave Captain Dave Severance's Company E idle, that unit was turned loose on bypassed Japanese emplacements to the rear of the 1st Battalion.)[19]

Company E's 3rd Platoon harbored a malcontent Marine named Donald Ruhl, a private first class who had fought in the Solomon Islands as a paramarine and who had been transferred to the 2nd Battalion, 28th Marines, to help stiffen its long roster of young men who had yet to see combat. As such, Ruhl was grudgingly and tacitly allowed to entertain the troops and troop leaders with a steady stream of complaints and minor stunts (including an iron-clad boycott against tooth brushing) that were designed to show management that it had better toe the line. But it was Ruhl who had to toe the line—had to show the way—by setting a positive example in the only true test of a Marine at war, in combat.

Ruhl

Donald Jack Ruhl was born on July 2, 1923, in Columbus, Montana, and was raised there until 1937, when he became a farmhand on a 40-acre farm in Joliet, Montana. He made $15 per week plus room and board until just after graduating from high school in May 1942, when he briefly worked as a laboratory assistant for a refining company.

Ruhl enlisted in the Marine Corps Reserve on September 12, 1942, and volunteered for jump school right out of boot camp. In due course, he was promoted private first class and assigned to the 3rd Parachute Battalion, then in training at Camp Elliott, California. When the battalion left San Diego for overseas duty, Ruhl went as a 60mm mortar crewman. Training resumed until just before the battalion was committed to the invasion of Bougainville at Empress Augusta Bay. It left Bougainville in January 1944 and was deactivated in February. When the former paramarines reached the United States, many were assigned to the 28th Marines, and Ruhl was sent to Company E.[20]

Wells

John Keith Wells was born on February 5, 1922, and raised in northern Texas. He attended Texas A&M College from 1940 until he dropped out to enlist in the Marine Corps in March 1942 and was soon slated to attend officer candidate school. After earning his commission, Second Lieutenant Wells attended jump school and thereafter joined the 1st Marine Parachute Regiment on Guadalcanal in December 1943—just in time to be shipped back to the United States when the paramarine program was terminated in February 1944. He was assigned upon his arrival at Camp Pendleton, California, to Company E, 28th Marines.

It was during the company's training cycle that Wells began to talk up Jenghis Khan as a role model. Referring to the Mongol leader's many military successes, Wells often chanted, "Give me fifty Marines not afraid to die and I can take any position." In fact, he was given more than forty Marines, with some certainly afraid to die even though they never said so.

The way his hand had been dealt, D-day at Iwo Jima was Keith Wells's first opportunity to put his theory to work, and to prove himself to his Marines.[21]

Wells and Ruhl

Though it remained apart from the rest of the 2nd Battalion to continue to serve as the 28th Marines' regimental reserve, Company E was given the

important assignment of maintaining contact between the struggling, grieving
1st Battalion and the regimental dumps being assembled under constant fire
on Beach Green. Among the duties the reserve company took upon itself
was checking and clearing defensive structures on the ground in its zone of
responsibility, structures loosely defined as "cleared" by the 1st Battalion.[22]

One such structure in the zone being held by Company E's 3rd Platoon was
a quite large, earth-covered mound suspected of harboring a large artillery piece
and more than enough Japanese to man it. Complicating a straightforward
assault on the position was the presence of two dying 1st Battalion Marines
presumably left beside the bunker to be treated by a follow-on wave of rear-area
specialists, including graves registration and field medical personnel. The bunker
could not be blown up without endangering the two mortally wounded Marines
and their platoon leader, who had elected to remain with them to the bitter end.

The 3rd Platoon leader did not like having a fully manned Japanese artillery
piece sequestered near his troops. Wells sounded an urgent note when he told a
demolitions assault man to prepare to deliver a bunker-demolishing charge. He
also asked the young 1st Battalion lieutenant to round up some 1st Battalion
troops to move the dying Marines to a place of safety. There was a brief argument
between the lieutenants, but the 1st Battalion man ultimately complied.

Before anyone quite knew what was going on, there arrived on the scene
a 1st Battalion captain who had overheard the lieutenants exchange their
views. He opined that the bunker was nothing more lethal than a "supply
house," and he ordered Lieutenant Wells to move his platoon closer to the
1st Battalion perimeter. This Wells did—all of 25 yards—and set his troops
on a line facing the putative supply house.

Content with the placement of his 3rd Platoon, Lieutenant Wells gripped his
signature .45-caliber Thompson submachine gun, and motioned Private First
Class Don Ruhl to join him as he inspected the many patches of shell-spattered
scrubwood that might be hiding Japanese infiltrators or stragglers. Ruhl, who
was wearing his fatigue cover in place of his discarded helmet, hefted his M1
rifle and closely followed Wells.

As Wells and Ruhl kicked through the scrubwood, the bunker came to life.
A concrete door facing to the southwest slid open and the muzzle of a 75mm
field gun poked through and fired. Before Wells could do anything, a squad
of 1st Battalion Marines charged to the fore until one of them was killed and
the rest were stymied by machine-gun fire from the bunker.

Suddenly, a Marine appeared atop the bunker. He set a shape charge and
departed. The charge was not powerful enough to kill the occupants of the
bunker, but it was sufficient to blow a hole through the roof.

As the 75mm gun ceased firing and the concrete door was shut tight, another Marine bounded to the top of the bunker and dropped a thermite grenade through the new hole in the roof. The heat and smoke from the grenade was soon killing many of the occupants, and the others tried to flee through a second concrete door that faced directly toward Wells and Ruhl.

As the white smoke from the thermite grenade was vented via the newly opened door, eight Japanese charged into the open, intent upon legging it to friendly lines. When Wells spotted them, he raised his Thompson and fired off an entire 40-round magazine. At the same time, Ruhl emptied his eight-round M1 clip.

Three Japanese dropped from bullet strikes while the other five fled. Without much thought, Ruhl charged forward with his bayonet pointed at the escapees, skewered one of them and shot another.[23]

Wells noticed that a hand grenade was arcing from a thicket of scrubwood—directly toward Ruhl. He yelled a warning at which Ruhl dropped flat on the ground and evaded the spray of shrapnel.

Lieutenant Wells was on the prowl despite the fact that dusk was falling. He seated a fresh magazine into his Thompson and broke cover to go after the unseen grenadier in the hope the man had resorted to tossing a grenade because he had no rifle or pistol. The risk never paid off; after coming up emptyhanded from thrashing around in the thicket, Wells withdrew to the 3rd Platoon line.

Wells had been dubbed "Jenghiz Khan" during the regiment's training days, when he often promulgated the lessons of the great conqueror's military campaigns to the troops. It all sounded like bravado to those young men (of whom several were older than the lofty 23-year-old lieutenant), but the proof of Wells's claim on leadership was given in spades on D-day evening on Iwo Jima.

So too did the 3rd Platoon's resident malcontent validate his ticket as a stand-up combat Marine. That very evening, Ruhl asked to be assigned as Wells's permanent runner, and Wells instantly agreed. The two had been bonded in the blood of their nation's enemies.[24]

Shut Down

The entire ad hoc 28th Marines' plan shut down at around dusk. The two-company attack never had the strength or heavy weapons support it needed to remotely achieve a breakthrough.[25] Nevertheless, for all that the 28th Marines ran out of steam by dusk, it was the first of eight regimental combat teams on Iwo Jima to reach its D-day objectives: Suribachi and its garrison were isolated by the time the sun went down. Moreover, the combat team as a whole was in a good position to consolidate the ground it already held and to expand its holdings around the volcano's base once it was able to sort itself out in the wake of horrendous D-day chaos and loss.

Rosenthal

Joseph John Rosenthal, was born in Washington, D.C., on October 9, 1911. He became enamored of photography when he was twelve: "[I] became a photographer because [I] had saved cigar-store coupons and, looking through the catalogue, realized [I] couldn't get the prizes [I] wanted because [I] did not have enough coupons, and so took a camera instead."[26]

In 1930, a year after Rosenthal graduated from high school in Washington, D.C., he moved to San Francisco and landed a job as an office boy for the Newspaper Enterprise Association, the first syndicate founded (in 1902 by Edward Willis Scripps) to supply feature stories, illustrations, and cartoons to newspapers.[27]

Young Rosenthal next found a dream job in 1932 as a reporter-photographer with the *San Francisco News.* Eight years later, in 1940, as the United States' entry into World War II loomed, he attempted to win a spot in the U.S. Army Signal Corps photography program, but he was rejected owing to extremely poor eyesight. He attended the University of San Francisco for the 1941 school year, then joined the Associated Press's San Francisco photography staff. In 1943, he served as a United States Maritime Service photographer and traveled to Great Britain and North Africa. Rosenthal went back to work for AP in March 1944 as a member of the Wartime Still Pictures Pool covering the Pacific front. There he documented U.S. Marine Corps and U.S. Army island invasions at Hollandia, New Guinea; Guam, in the Mariana Islands; and Peleliu and Angaur in the Palau Islands.[28]

Rosenthal, though a minor player, was recognized by his peers and photo editors at newspapers around the United States as having fully developed his own intimate style of war photography. He was considered a very good—and courageous—photographer with a distinctive style that owed much to his attention to compositional detail.

In January 1945, Rosenthal was at Pearl Harbor, waiting for a big operation at an unknown location to begin. Over the course of a three-week wait, as he looked on in awe, many of the great names in Pacific War journalism arrived to fill out the invasion press corps. Assignments were handed out just before the journalists needed to load aboard ship. And all the newsmen were given the first official word about the target—a volcanic island named Iwo Jima, located in the tiny Volcano Islands group, about 600 miles south of Tokyo at the farthest frontier of the Japanese home islands.[29]

Joe Rosenthal left Hawaii aboard the ship that was carrying the veteran 4th Marine Division's 2nd Battalion, 24th Marines, to Iwo, but he decided he needed to get ashore earlier than it would take the veteran battalion to get ashore. At a stopover at Saipan, the pool photographer asked a public information officer to find him a more suitable infantry unit to accompany ashore. Always willing to accommodate newsmen, the officer only had to hear the photographer say, "It's the difference between getting the pictures I want, and not getting them." With that, Rosenthal was transferred to the transport carrying the veteran 2nd Battalion, 25th Marines, which was scheduled to land one to three hours into the assault on the northeasternmost landing beach.

Unremitting Japanese fire upon the landing beaches and terrible inshore sailing conditions caused a huge pile-up of traffic on and approaching the island as the avenues of approach became clogged with shattered amtracs and landing craft and stalled, often wrecked, wheeled vehicles and not a few tracked vehicles. But after five hours of idling offshore in a landing craft filled with mortar ammunition, Rosenthal was dumped on the beach with an infantry company headquarters party. By then the main event had moved inland in the face of non-stop artillery, mortar, machine-gun, and rifle fire, but the gunfire sweeping the busy beaches had not noticeably diminished.

Wading from seawater to wet loose sand that gave booted feet little purchase was a skill gained and set aside: the impetus of gunfire fostered quick learning as the Marines Rosenthal was accompanying hotfooted it inland, to a relatively mild band of beachhead real estate between the beach and the front line. Wreckage intermingled with dead and broken American bodies marked the progress of the advance every bloody step of the way. The overtaxed graves registration troops and engineers were still sanitizing the beach, had not yet ventured inland.

Rosenthal took several photos on the beach, but the favored viewpoint of a burning ammunition jeep was unattainable owing to sweeping gunfire, so the finicky cameraman let it go. In search of a scene he could immortalize without risking mortal danger, Rosenthal raced forward in the wake of a pair of Marines.

The photographer was closing on four feet behind the pair when he heard a *clank* and saw one of the Marines topple clumsily to the volcanic soil, dead from a round through his helmet. In a few more strides, Rosenthal and the surviving Marine hurled themselves into the shell hole they had risked all to reach.

And here is where we witness Joe Rosenthal's unique, effective but finicky style of picture taking:

Rosenthal had his head down while catching his breath, but he nonetheless spotted a dead Marine leaning up against the wall of a shallow shell crater, sprawled in such a way as to suggest that he had been running while holding his rifle out of ahead of him as he attacked a Japanese position.

As it dawned on Rosenthal that he could not get the sort of photo he wanted from where he was, he circled around the dead Marine, leapfrogging from shell crater to shell crater, to locate a better—preferably the perfect—viewpoint. When he found that, he stood up, exposed to anyone who had the means to kill him. It was then that he noticed that a second dead Marine was sprawled in a crater that would be in the photo he wanted to take. But, even then, the shot was not complete. The photographer sensed that another element was needed to complete the scene he found in his mind's eye—and that other element was a living Marine transiting the view. When his need was met Rosenthal released the shutter and immediately plopped down in a shell crater, mission accomplished.

Over the course of the eleven days he spent on Iwo Jima, Joe Rosenthal took 65 photographs, of which most were routine fare for American news outlets and several just plain didn't have any value. One, however, one that was one in ten million, would be an authentic, enduring masterpiece that elevated Joe Rosenthal to mythic status.[30]

Long before the 5th Marine Division left Hawaii for Iwo Jima, Private Philip Ward, a member of Company E's 3rd Platoon Assault Squad, had become used to the sound of gunfire over the course of many live-fire exercises. Every American on Beach Green was used to the sound and fury of gunfire. But only when the Japanese opened fire on Beach Green on D-day morning was Phil Ward—and every other American combat virgin on Iwo Jima—brought face-to-face with an industrialized level of *hostile,* intentionally lethal gunfire that drove him and many others to think of and even blurt out a new hitherto unrealized truth: "They're shooting at me."[31] And so it went.

If they had been polled that night, every American who had risked his life going ashore on Iwo Jima during D-day would have given the same answer to this question: What did you learn about war today? That answer would have been: Death in war is random.

Following minute analysis after the battle, a record-setting total of 501 Americans were found to have been randomly killed on Iwo Jima just on D-day, February 19, 1945. A further 47 died of wounds, 18 went missing, another 1,755 were wounded,[32] and 99 went down with "war neurosis"—combat fatigue.[33]

Dramatis Personae

Harlon Block

René Gagnon

John Bradley

James Forrestal

Bob Campbell

Bill Genaust

Hank Hansen

Ira Hayes

Ray Jacobs

Chandler Johnson

Norm Hatch

Chuck Lindberg

Lou Lowery

Joe Rosenthal

Donald Ruhl

Phil Ward

Harold Schultz

Harry Liversedge

Mike Strank

Ernest "Boots" Thomas

Dave Severance

Franklin Sousley

Harold "George" Schrier

John "Keith" Wells

Alexander A. Vandegrift

CHAPTER 3

Operation Hot Rocks

February 20 – D+1

The fanatical Japanese mass suicide attack nearly every American on Iwo Jima thought of as a sure thing never materialized. Relief was tempered by the knowledge that, as scary and fraught as such an attack might be, killing Japanese in the open was way better than prying them out of each and every one of their mutually supporting defensive emplacements.

Suribachi

By dusk on D-day, the 5th Marine Division's 28th Marines had traversed from Beach Green, on the V Amphibious Corps' extreme left flank, all the way across Iwo's narrow neck. By dawn on February 20, the regiment—reinforced by a tank company, now at half strength following a murderous trip from Beach Green to the front lines; a 105mm howitzer battalion, landed and dug-in during the late afternoon of February 19; an engineer company; and a detachment of experimental rocket-launcher trucks—faced two directions. While Lieutenant Colonel Jackson Butterfield's battered 1st Battalion faced north in a blocking position, Lieutenant Colonel Charles Shepard's 3rd Battalion and Lieutenant Colonel Chandler Johnson's 2nd Battalion faced south and west, toward Suribachi, the regimental objective.[1]

Until the 556-foot-high volcano was defanged and completely in its hands, the 28th Marines would fight under an operational plan dubbed "Hot Rocks," a battle distinct from the V Amphibious Corps' much larger northward drive to capture Iwo Jima's three airfields.

The terrain to the south of the 28th Marines line was largely open, strewn with large boulders thrown out by the volcano, impeded by gullies and folds, and guarded by hundreds of bunkers, pillboxes, caves, and other fighting emplacements, most of them on high ground overlooking all the land approaches to Iwo Jima's premier fortress. It was an apocalyptic landscape, churned by countless shellings and bombings over the 74-day run-up to D-day.

Then there was the volcano itself, isolated, brooding, sheer in many places, serviced by only a handful of footpaths, and completely dominant above the land approaches.

As follow-on units of the 5th Marine Division arrived ashore on D+1, the 1st Battalion, 28th Marines, was placed in regimental reserve to allow it to reorganize, and the rest of the combat team made ready to jump off into light but persistent rain showers.

H-hour was 0830, February 20. The entire 2nd Battalion—including Company E, freshly released from the regimental reserve—was on the left, with the 3rd Battalion on the right.

The plan was to fully invest the base of the volcano in order to divert its firepower away from the main V Amphibious Corps attack to the northwest, to isolate and fix its garrison, and then to attack uphill—through the rain if need be—to the summit. As soon as the infantry attack jumped off, many of the regimental combat team's crew-served weapons—artillery, mortars, antitank guns, rocket trucks, tanks, and medium machine guns—would attempt to blot out Japanese weapons set in on the volcano.[2]

It was chilly and drizzling when the attack opened with a carrier air strike that included napalm, bombs, and rockets, then a heavy bombardment by Marine artillery and naval gunfire. Access to direct artillery and naval support was all good news. Balancing it, however, was the bad news that the eight surviving medium gun and flame tanks of 16 sent ashore with Company C, 5th Tank Battalion, were experiencing supply-chain problems and would be delayed indefinitely until fuel and ammunition reached them. This was accomplished in time for the tanks to advance alongside the infantry beginning at about 1100 hours.[3]

As soon as they stepped off, the Marine infantrymen faced terrific fire from scores of gun emplacements, many heretofore silent, or at least uncharted. Gains through the morning were 50 to 70 yards. Coarse, ashy mud was everywhere, so thick that, when it inevitably infiltrated weapons, the rate of fire was reduced to one round at a time, a serious diminution of offensive firepower.

Even the throttling of gunfire—and the resulting lower ammunition usage—caused by the coarse mud did not alter the fact that the fighting was at such close quarters that the only way to bring up ammunition was to dispatch it in on the only adaptable conveyances available: on the backs and in the arms of individual Marines.

Ruhl

At approximately 1130, while Company E was still sitting on its hands waiting for orders to join the front-line action, Private First Class Donald Ruhl jumped into the antitank ditch that was shielding the company command group and approached the first sergeant to request permission to mount a rescue mission to retrieve a Marine who had been wounded and immobilized about 40 yards in front of the company's front line. Both men knew that an earlier rescue attempt had been driven off by a Japanese machine gun that wounded several Americans. Nevertheless, after the first sergeant advised Ruhl of the facts, he gave the aggressive young Marine permission to make the effort.

Ruhl climbed out of the antitank ditch and ran toward the wounded man, thus triggering a considerable volume of small-arms and machine-gun fire aimed at him. For all the gunfire, Ruhl reached the wounded man without being shot.

Without waiting for a lull, Ruhl dragged and then carried the fellow Marine back to the antitank ditch, where he commandeered a litter and a Marine to help him lug it through more heavy fire to the 2nd Battalion aid station, which was 300 yards farther back and marked by a rifle upended and pinned to the earth by its bayonet. As soon as the wounded Marine was safely delivered, Ruhl charged back through heavy gunfire to resume his firing position on the Company E front line.[4]

Bunker Busting

Fighting throughout the day took place largely at arm's-length distances. Most often, when a Japanese emplacement was spotted, an infantry squad laid on heavy suppressive fire with its hand-held weapons. If a tank was near enough, efforts were made to bring its 75mm main gun or flame gun to bear. Or a 75mm halftrack-mounted antitank gun or 37mm antitank gun might attempt to fire rounds through firing embrasures and entryways. If not, a flamethrower team moved up to blot out a hopefully unmanned portal or embrasure with one or two powerful spurts of flaming napalm. Then infantrymen moved up to toss grenades inside. And, finally, a demolitions team blew up the emplacement. Later, when the area had been cleared, engineers utterly demolished each overrun position to deny its use to infiltrators. It was slow, courageous work, and many Marines died in its service.[5]

Company E

As soon as Company E was released from the regimental reserve, just after the morning attack was launched, it had to hike back over a lot of the ground it had traversed on D-day. Then, while the rest of the battalion sought to advance toward the volcano, the company was placed to the rear as the 2nd Battalion reserve.[6]

Becoming impatient from having to sit on his hands, Company E's skipper, Captain Dave Severance, sent his 1st Platoon into a limited local attack that quickly resulted in the loss of the platoon leader, who was wounded. It took until around 1600 hours for Company E, less its 1st Platoon, to be committed to the 2nd Battalion's main, nearly stalled, attack. The company's task was to relieve a 2nd Battalion unit that had taken a very high volume of casualties.

By the time Company E moved forward to join the battalion assault, the 2nd Battalion, 28th Marines, had managed to advance all of a hundred yards from the day's line of departure. By the time it replaced the other unit, the sun was behind the volcano and a huge shadow obscured the view to the west. Light out or dark, the bloody attack toward Suribachi resumed with a new cast and ground forward incrementally, at the methodical rate of the by-the-book bunker-busting technique the 28th Marines had learned in its year of training.

Bradley

As soon as Company E had been committed to the 2nd Battalion front line, Pharmacist's Mate John Bradley swept into action to save the lives of any wounded or injured Marine he could find on his own or heard about. He was completely focused on his life-saving mission—so much so that the battalion surgeon eventually waylaid him as he passed through the open-air aid station and suggested he take a break and help the station staff for a while. Doc Bradley admitted that he was bushed, but he protested that he simply could not leave wounded comrades out on the battlefield.[7]

> Edward S. Pennell
> Navy Cross Citation:
> The President of the United States takes pleasure in presenting the Navy Cross to Edward S. Pennell (0-30461), Second Lieutenant, U.S. Marine Corps (Reserve), for extraordinary heroism as a Rifle Platoon Leader of Company E, Second Battalion, Twenty-Eighth Marines, FIFTH Marine Division, in action against enemy Japanese forces on Iwo Jima, Volcano

Islands, 20 February 1945. Boldly defying intense enemy fire to attempt a rescue of five wounded men who were inaccessible to litter bearers and in need of immediate medical attention, Second Lieutenant Pennell ran one hundred yards to a tank and, by the use of the tank telephone, guided it into a position adjacent to two of the more seriously wounded men. After his men[8] had placed the two wounded Marines in a small trench, he directed the movement of the tank until it straddled the casualties, enabling the wounded men to be pulled into the tank through the escape hatch in the floor. Still exposed to heavy hostile fire, he guided the vehicle through his platoon's entrenchments to a tank road. Then, contacting a second tank, he repeated the rescue operations to remove two more seriously wounded men and, when the first tank returned to the front, succeeded in evacuating the fifth casualty. By his daring initiative and courage under fire, Second Lieutenant Pennell undoubtedly saved the lives of five of his men. His leadership throughout was in keeping with the highest traditions of the United States Naval Service.

Ruhl

Only one heroic act on D+1 does not appear to have been satisfying enough for the 3rd Platoon's leading malcontent, so Donald Ruhl had to go out of his way to find further satisfaction.

During the last hours of the day's assault toward Suribachi, Ruhl and a buddy presented themselves to the 3rd Platoon's Lieutenant Keith Wells to tell him that there appeared to be a Japanese field gun a short way to the front that could not be reduced by friendly artillery or mortars because seven wounded Marines were on the ground too close to allow the gun to be blasted to ruin, and that the gun position might or might not be manned. The pair volunteered to see whether the gun was manned or not, and Wells accepted the offer.

As many mostly stymied Marines looked on, Ruhl and his buddy took off over open ground in the face of sheets of gunfire that had proven fatal or debilitating to many Marines. They both survived unscathed and tumbled into the above-ground gun emplacement to see for themselves that it had been abandoned.

Darkness had engulfed the area and rescuing any of the seven wounded Marines nearby was too dangerous, even for Ruhl. The pair decided to remain in the emplacement in order to deny its gunners use of the weapon in case they returned   to conduct a night bombardment of the Marine lines or rear area.[9]

By 1700 hours, when the day's work ended, the 2nd and 3rd battalions had advanced about 200 yards at the cost of 29 killed and 133 wounded.

As night fell, the Japanese on Suribachi fired signal flares to request that artillery and mortar fire be placed on the attackers, who ended the day in positions well short of the base of the mountain.[10]

Ruhl

In the middle of the second night ashore, Private First Class Donald Ruhl decided he simply had to explore a cave near the abandoned Japanese field gun emplacement that he and a buddy had occupied, to see if it might be harboring any live Japanese. Leaving his buddy in the gun emplacement and using individual kitchen matches for light, Ruhl followed the cave to its end, found no one, commandeered several woolen blankets, and returned unmolested to the field gun emplacement.[11]

February 21 – D+2

At 0730 on February 21, which featured more cold rain and strong winds that threw up a six-foot surf, the reinforced 28th Marines hunkered down as heavy preparatory fire screamed overhead against known Japanese emplacements and designated area targets. Just before the scheduled 0800 resumption of the ground attack, 40 carrier fighters and bombers attacked to within a scary 100 yards of the friendly infantry with machine guns, rockets, and bombs. After waiting in vain for refueled tanks to come forward to support them, the attacking infantry—now including the somewhat restored 1st Battalion, 28th Marines, in a column of companies deployed on the extreme right—finally jumped off at 0825. Naval gunfire was placed as needed ahead of the troops.[12]

Company E

One of the first Marines to respond to the order to get up and go was Lieutenant Keith Wells, leading Company E's 3rd Platoon. Wells simply rose to his feet, waved his heavy Thompson submachine gun toward the mountain, and stalked forward without uttering a word, leading only by his usual courageous example. Lieutenant Ed Pennell, Company E's 2nd Platoon leader, did pretty much the same. And so did hundreds of 2nd Battalion men, who followed the platoon leaders' bold example.[13]

And then the whole mountain erupted in gunfire and shellfire, right in the faces of those hundreds of exposed Marines. Among the many wounded was the 3rd Platoon's Corporal Dick Wheeler, who would chronicle the first four days on Iwo in his excellent book, *The Bloody Battle for Suribachi*. And the 3rd Platoon's Pharmacist's Mate Third Class Clifford Langley, who was treating Wheeler for a facial wound when another mortar round fell close by and wounded both of them. Wheeler was evacuated owing to terrific blood loss, but Langley ignored his own bleeding wounds, commandeered Wheeler's rifle, and went on to find more lives to save.[14]

Ruhl

Diverging somewhat from the route taken by Lieutenant Keith Wells, the 3rd Platoon's heroic Private First Class Donald Ruhl joined the platoon guide, Sergeant Henry "Hank" Hansen, in a race to the base of the volcano, where a fringe of brush had been shell-blasted sufficiently to reveal unearthed corners of a clutch of sand-covered pillboxes and bunkers. Gunfire from within and around the reinforced-concrete fighting positions drove Ruhl and Hansen to ground atop a blasted pillbox. Both Marines fired off whatever bullets their rifles carried at the most immediate danger, a handful of Japanese getting ready to put grenades to work.

One grenade landed between Ruhl and Hansen. Ruhl—who had time to clear out—made a split-second decision to save the sergeant, who was exposed in the center of the pillbox's roof. Bellowing "Look out, Hank,"[15] Ruhl leaped atop the grenade and died instantly as he allowed his abdomen to absorb the entire fury of the grenade's detonation.[16]

Private First Class Donald J. Ruhl, USMCR
Medal of Honor Citation:
For conspicuous gallantry and intrepidity at the risk of his life above and beyond the call of duty while serving as a Rifleman in an Assault Platoon of Company E, Twenty-eight Marines, Fifth Marine Division, in action against enemy Japanese Forces on Iwo Jima, Volcano Islands, from 19 to 21 February 1945. Quick to press the advantage after eight Japanese had been driven from a blockhouse on D-Day, Private First Class Ruhl singlehandedly attacked the group, killing one of the enemy with his bayonet and another by rifle fire in his determined attempt to annihilate the escaping troops. Cool and undaunted as the fury of hostile resistance steadily increased throughout the night, he voluntarily left the shelter of his tank trap early in the morning of D-Day plus 1 and moved out under tremendous volume of mortar and machine-gun fire to rescue a wounded Marine lying in an exposed position approximately forty yards forward of the line. Half pulling and half carrying the wounded man, he removed him to a defoliated position, called for an assistant and a stretcher and, again running the gauntlet of hostile fire, carried the casualty to an Aid Station some three hundred yards distant on the beach. Returning to his platoon, he continued his valiant efforts, volunteering to investigate an apparently abandoned Japanese gun emplacement seventy-five yards forward of the flank during consolidation of the front lines, and subsequently occupying the position through the night to prevent the enemy from repossessing the valuable weapon. Pushing forward in the assault against the vast network of fortifications surrounding Mt. Suribachi the following morning, he crawled with his platoon guide to the top of a Japanese bunker to bring fire to bear on enemy troops located on the far side of the bunker, [when] suddenly a

hostile grenade landed between the two Marines. Instantly Private First Class Ruhl called a warning to his fellow Marine and dived on the deadly missile, absorbing the full impact of the shattering explosion in his own body and protecting all within range from the danger of flying fragments although he might easily have dropped from his position on the edge of the bunker to the ground below. An indomitable fighter, Private First Class Ruhl rendered heroic service toward to defeat of a ruthless enemy, and his valor, initiative and unfaltering spirit of self-sacrifice in the face of almost certain death sustained and enhanced the highest traditions of the United States Naval Service. He gallantly gave his life his country.

Bradley

Pharmacist's Mate John Bradley went into his usual combat overdrive the moment a Marine fell wounded within reach. He never stopped as long as Americans were still bleeding.

> Pharmacist's Mate 2nd Class John H. Bradley, USNR
>
> Navy Cross Citation:
>
> For extraordinary heroism in action against the enemy at Iwo Jima on Feb. 21, 1945 as a hospital corpsman attached to a Marine Rifle platoon. During a furious assault by his company upon a strongly defended enemy zone at the base of Mt. Suribachi, Bradley observed a Marine infantryman fall wounded in an open area under a pounding barrage by mortars, interlaced with a merciless crossfire from Machine guns. With complete disregard for his own safety, he ran through the intense fire to the side of the fallen Marine, examined his wounds and ascertained that an immediate administration of plasma was necessary to save the man's life. Unwilling to subject any of his comrades to the danger to which he had so valiantly exposed himself, he signaled would-be assistants to remain where they were. Placing himself in a position to shield the wounded man, he tied a plasma unit to a rifle planted upright in the sand and continued his life saving mission. The Marine's wounds bandaged and the condition of shock relieved by plasma, Bradley pulled the man thirty yards through intense enemy fire to a position of safety. His indomitable spirit, dauntless initiative, and heroic devotion to duty were an inspiration to those with whom he served and were in keeping with the highest tradition of the United States Naval Service.

Wells

Lieutenant Keith Wells, still at the forefront of Company E's 3rd Platoon, got a little ahead of the platoon to his left and was thus exposed to direct gunfire from that flank as well as the usual danger from dead ahead. In short order, the opposing fire became so intense that Company E was pinned down, especially by grenades and automatic weapons fire from a bunker. Flamethrowers were needed, and the 3rd Platoon's Corporal Chuck Lindberg and Private Robert Goode hotfooted it to the front in response to Wells's urgent call. For all their willingness to close with the enemy, the mortar fire protecting the bunker was too intense to breast. As several Marines discussed options, a mortar shell burst nearby, wounding five. Lieutenant Wells sustained numerous shrapnel wounds in his legs, which he chose to ignore. Even so, Doc Bradley arrived at his platoon leader's side and injected him with a dose of pain-killing morphine and, in strong terms, prescribed evacuation, advice Wells ignored even though he had no feeling in his legs.

The lieutenant's brave example drove Lindberg and Goode to decisive action. Both flamethrower operators breasted the ongoing intense mortar barrage all the way to the bunker and doused the position with burning napalm until they ran out of fuel. (Each 72-pound tank carried six seconds' worth of fuel.) By then, the smell of burning flesh and exploding ammunition in the bunker and throughout a web of interconnected pillboxes threatened to cause Lindberg and Goode to withdraw.

Though wobbly, Keith Wells remained determined to stay with his troops. The morphine administered by Doc Bradley was reducing the pain, but he could feel his legs well enough to get around.

Wells more or less collapsed a little before noon. The fall opened up many of his blood-encrusted leg wounds and the fresh bleeding left him feeling weak and exhausted. Doc Bradley arrived to administer another dose of morphine and then bandaged Wells's many open wounds.[17]

Keith Wells's heroic fighting spirit kept him at the front for another 30-odd minutes, but he knew he was going downhill and decided to turn the 3rd Platoon over to his highly competent second-in-command, Platoon Sergeant Ernest "Boots" Thomas. Wells crawled to the battalion aid station under his own power.[18]

First Lieutenant John K. Wells, USMCR
Navy Cross Citation:
The President of the United States takes pleasure in presenting the Navy Cross to John K. Wells (0-21592), First Lieutenant, U.S. Marine Corps (Reserve), for extraordinary heroism as a Rifle Platoon Leader of Company E, Second Battalion, Twenty-Eighth Marines, FIFTH Marine Division, in action against enemy Japanese forces on Iwo Jima, Volcano Islands, 21 February 1945. When ordered to attack across open terrain and dislodge the enemy from a series of strongly-defended pillboxes and blockhouses at the base of Mount Suribachi, First Lieutenant Wells placed himself in the forefront of his platoon and, leading his men forward in the face of intense hostile machine-gun, mortar and rifle fire, continuously moved from one flank to the other to lead assault groups one by one in their attacks on Japanese emplacements. Although severely wounded while directing his demolition squad in an assault on a formidable enemy blockhouse whose fire had stopped the advance of his platoon, he continued to lead his men until the blockhouse was destroyed. When, an hour later, the pain from his wound became so intense that he was no longer able to walk, he established his

command post in a position from which to observe the progress of his men and continued to control their attack by means of messengers. By his courageous leadership and indomitable fighting spirit, First Lieutenant Wells contributed materially to the destruction of at least twenty-five Japanese emplacements, and his unwavering devotion to duty was in keeping with the highest traditions of the United States Naval Service.

Counter-Counterattack

During the late afternoon, the pilot of a U.S. Navy observation plane flying a routine mission over Suribachi noted that a crowd of Japanese appeared to be forming up for a counterattack on the center of the sector of the 2nd Battalion, 28th Marines—the portion of front-line real estate held by Company E.

It took only a matter of minutes for ground controllers and close-air-support teams to organize an aerial intervention. Soon, fighter-bombers roared in from the Marine rear toward the gathering Japanese. Each American plane dropped its bombs, fired its air-to-ground rockets, and strafed the mountain, then pulled up to make way for the next plane.

It took a few moments for the intense noise of explosions and hammering machine guns to dissipate, and then members of Company E's 2nd Platoon rose from their cover and swelled forward. At the forefront of the Marines was Sergeant Michael Strank, a squad leader who had enlisted in the Marine Corps in 1939. A natural leader and heroic by nature, Strank got the men around him revved up by shouting at the top of his lungs: "Let's show these bastards what a real banzai is like! Easy Company, charge!"[19]

Mike Strank's example set off a foot race to the base of the volcano by men who moments earlier had been bone-tired wraiths, exhausted by their travails and beaten down by the death and bloodletting all around them.

In its turn, the 2nd Platoon's assault led by Strank set an example for the 3rd Platoon's new leader, Platoon Sergeant Ernest Thomas.

Thomas

Ernest Ivy "Boots" Thomas, Jr., was born on March 10, 1924, in Tampa and raised in Monticello, Florida. At 17, Thomas was working toward a degree in aeronautical engineering at Indiana's Tri-State University when he decided, shortly after the Japanese attack on Pearl Harbor, to drop out to enlist in the Marine Corps. Unfortunately, Thomas suffered from colorblindness, which would have eliminated him at that time for active duty in any United States military branch, but Thomas had a plan to get around the test during his pre-induction physical: he asked the enlistee sitting next to him at the testing station to tell him which colors showed up where on the test diagram, and he memorized the entire chart. He passed the test and was sworn in on May 27, 1942. When he graduated from boot camp at the Parris Island, South Carolina, recruit depot, Boots Thomas was retained as an instructor, a role he continued to fill after he was transferred to Camp Lejeune, North Carolina. He worked hard, showed a good aptitude for leadership, and rose through the ranks. In March 1944, Thomas was transferred to Camp Pendleton, California, with orders to the 28th Marines. The entire 5th Marine Division was dispatched to Camp Tarawa, Hawaii, on Hilo, in September 1944, and when it boarded ship for Iwo Jima in January 1945, Boots Thomas was the 20-year-old platoon sergeant for Company E's 3rd Platoon.[20]

Platoon Sergeant Ernest I. Thomas, Jr., USMCR
   Navy Cross Citation:
   The Navy Cross is presented posthumously to Ernest I. Thomas, Jr., United States Marine Corps Reserve, for extraordinary heroism as a Rifle Platoon Leader serving with Company E, Second Battalion, Twenty-Eighth Marines, Fifth Marine Division, during action on enemy Japanese-held Iwo Jima, Volcano Islands, 21 February 1945. When his platoon leader was wounded, Platoon Sergeant THOMAS assumed command and, before supporting tanks arrived to cover him, led his men in an assault on a fanatically defended and heavily fortified hostile sector at the base of Mount Suribachi. With the tanks unable to proceed over the rough terrain beyond positions 75 to 100 yards at the rear of our attacking forces, Platoon Sergeant Thomas ran repeatedly to the nearest tank, and in a position exposed to heavy and accurate machine-gun and mortar barrages, directed the fire of the tanks against the Japanese pillboxes which were retarding his platoon's advance. After each trip to the tanks, he returned to his men and led them in assaulting and neutralizing enemy emplacements, continuing to advance against the Japanese with a knife as his only weapon after the destruction of his rifle by hostile fire. Under his aggressive leadership, the platoon killed all the enemy in the sector and contributed materially to the eventual capture of Mount Suribachi. His daring initiative, fearless leadership and unwavering devotion to duty were inspiring to those with whom he served and reflect the highest credit upon Platoon Sergeant Thomas and the United States Naval Service.

Attack

Gains were minimal with the aid of 75mm assault guns until 1100, when 37mm antitank guns and several rocket trucks were committed. As a result of having support from adequate bunker-busting weapons, beginning at about noon, the 1st Battalion's Company A became the first Marine combat unit to reach the base of the volcano.[21]

In the regimental center, set to attack more or less westward along Suribachi's northern curve, the 3rd Battalion, 28th Marines, hit an immovable barrier when it jumped off, but at-first-tiny inroads spread and the battalion was soon making real but limited strides against increasingly fractured defensive positions. Beginning at 1145, the first Japanese counterattack of the battle was beaten back, and then the thinned and perhaps demoralized opposition was more easily overcome, especially after several tanks reported for duty beside 37mm and self-propelled 75mm antitank guns. By 1400 hours, the 3rd Battalion had drawn abreast the 1st at the base of Suribachi.[22] Japanese troops attacked the 3rd Battalion once again at about 1800 and succeeded in knocking back a portion of Company H about 15 yards.[23]

On the far left of the regiment, Lieutenant Colonel Chandler Johnson's 2nd Battalion was held to very small gains for most of the day in the face of unremitting heavy fire, but it eventually bulled through with the aid of tanks to join its sister battalions on a wide semicircular front just short of the base of the volcano. At about 1400, Company F, on the 2nd Battalion left, began to swing around the volcano's eastern flank preparatory to mounting a sweep of Tobiishi Point, Iwo Jima's southern promontory.

For gains ranging between 500 and 1,000 yards on D+2, the 28th Marines had given up 34 dead and 153 wounded—adding up with previous days' casualties to 25-percent losses in three days.

After the February 21 advance was halted, roving Marines poured gasoline into fissures from which they could hear voices, and set the fuel ablaze to the accompaniment of screams and cooking-off ammunition. This was about as brutal as infantry warfare can get. The Japanese to the north once again contributed artillery and mortar fire that forced the Marine hunters to seek cover.[24]

February 22 – D+3

February 22 dawned miserable and rainy. Overnight, the deluge had turned the volcanic ash to mush that yet again infiltrated and clogged the workings of weapons. The weather also kept air support grounded on the carrier decks, and visibility from warships' radar-controlled gun directors was impaired. On the plus side, after two days of resupply fiascoes, seven fully fueled and armed Sherman medium tanks were on hand at the front when the assault recommenced.[25]

Luck of the Draw

The hairsbreadth luck-of-the-draw difference between living and dying at any moment on Iwo Jima hovered on every American's mind long after the death of friends became routine. The high and the mighty were not exempted.

At the 28th Marines command post at around 0800, as the senior staff routinely gathered to guide its Marines into hopefully decisive closure on the base of the volcano, a light mortar barrage landed close by. Standing next to Colonel Harry Liversedge and Captain Fred Haynes, the regimental surgeon, Commander Daniel McCarthy, dropped dead as a tiny sliver of shrapnel lodged in his heart. The colonel, Haynes, and everyone else in the tent was untouched.[26]

Forward

In the regimental center, the 3rd Battalion, 28th Marines, lurched forward against Suribachi's northern face, cleaned out the last bunkers, pillboxes, and caves in its zone, before Company G dispatched a 15-man patrol westward to the island's southwestern extremity.[27] Similarly, as soon as all defensive structures in the 2nd Battalion zone had been cleared, a 15-man Company E patrol advanced to the same feature by going around the eastern face.[28] The volcano was thus more or less surrounded.

Most of 28th Marine Regiment spent February 22 dressing its lines and methodically taking out emplacements around the base of the volcano—so much so that the defensive establishment was reduced to an estimate of between 300 and 600 survivors by nightfall. A sergeant from the 3rd Battalion returned from an unsanctioned lone-wolf foray partway up the northern slope to report no signs of the defenders. Even though this intimated an opportunity to scale some of the high ground quickly and cheaply, Colonel Liversedge decided it was by then too late in the day for the 3rd Battalion to advance and then properly dig in.[29]

Colonel Liversedge did plan to dispatch a strong patrol up the only remotely walkable route to the summit the next day, D+4, as soon as it was light enough to climb the often extremely steep path.

CHAPTER 4

The First Flag

Patrols

The assault on Suribachi itself jumped off in the pre-dawn hours of D+4: Friday, February 23, 1945. Aerial reconnaissance and photography conducted before, during, and after the invasion landings suggested that there remained, following massive shelling and bombing, only one practical route up the face of the volcano—and so only Lieutenant Colonel Chandler Johnson's 2nd Battalion, 28th Marines, was designated to step off. The other two battalions scoured their zones for Japanese-manned fighting emplacements they had thus far missed or intentionally bypassed.

The first Marines to test the waters for opposition from the Japanese still holding the summit of the volcano were 15 members of two squads from the 2nd Platoon, Company E, 28th Marines. Private First Class Ira Hayes, an automatic rifleman, describes the brief foray: "It was the morning of [February] 23rd that an order came from [Captain Severance] to send a [15]-man combat patrol clear around the base of Suribachi. Our whole squad was chosen, including [Corporal Harlon] Block, [Sergeant Michael] Strank, [Private First Class Franklin] Sousley, & myself, & another squad also. Well, we set out from our company CP, which was on the east side of Suribachi, & went south to encircle the volcano & wind up of the west side of Suribachi. Thank God we did not encounter any Japs on this patrol. We then returned to our company CP"[1]

The next Marines to move out of the 28th Marines lines—a four-man patrol composed of Company F's Sergeant Sherman Watson, Private Louis Charlo, Private Theodore White, and Private George Mercer—did so by 0800 hours. The four climbed and hiked—even ran—all the way to the summit, where they encountered an unmanned heavy machine-gun strongpoint at the rim of the crater. Ready ammunition was neatly laid out and the position was shipshape, but no one was home. Overall, a week of intense bombardment on these heights had made a tangle of blasted bunkers, pillboxes, and strewn weapons, gear, and supplies. There was no sign of a living being, so the patrol headed downslope at its best pace. Mission accomplished.[2]

Next, while the four-man Watson patrol was still reconnoitering a route to Suribachi's summit, Lieutenant Colonel Johnson sent off two three-man patrols, one each from Company D and Company F, to locate other possible routes.[3] And right after that, Johnson asked Company E's Captain Dave Severance to assemble a patrol of platoon strength with which he planned to send an American flag to the summit.[4]

With his 1st and 2nd platoons otherwise engaged,[5] Severance designated the now-24-man 3rd Platoon of Company E, (down from 45 men on D-day). The patrol leader was, at Colonel Harry Liversedge's specific request, the Company E executive officer, a 29-year-old mustang (officer commissioned from the ranks), First Lieutenant Harold George Schrier. (Liversedge had worked with fellow former Marine Raider Schrier in the central Solomon Islands.) According to Captain Severance, "[Schrier] was outstanding. He knew what to do and he took a lot of the load off [me]."[6]

Schrier

Harold George Schrier, the Company E, 28th Marines, executive officer, was born on October 17, 1916, in Corder, Missouri. He enlisted in the Marine Corps at 20 years of age on November 12, 1936, and graduated from Marine Corps Recruit Depot, San Diego. Private Schrier's first posting was to the U.S. Embassy Guard in Peking, China; he also served in Tientsin and Shanghai. He was selected as a drill instructor and reported aboard Marine Corps Recruit Depot, San Diego, in August 1940. Early in 1942, Sergeant Schrier volunteered for service with Lieutenant Colonel Evans Carlson's 2nd Raider Battalion, then training near San Diego; he was rapidly selected for promotion to platoon sergeant in April. Two companies of Carlson's Raiders, including Platoon Sergeant Schrier, were rushed to Midway in June 1942 to defend against a Japanese amphibious assault, but the invasion fleet was turned back following a momentous carrier-versus-carrier battle. Schrier next participated in the 2nd Raider Battalion's "Long Patrol" on Guadalcanal, an epic two-month ordeal of jungle warfare behind Japanese lines. Schrier distinguished himself when he led fellow Marines to safety after being cut off from friendly troops. This earned him a field promotion to second lieutenant in early 1943, and he was detached from the 2nd Raiders to take part in scouting and reconnoitering Japanese holdings in the central

Solomon Islands, for which he was awarded a Legion of Merit. Lieutenant Schrier returned to the United States in February 1944 to serve as an infantry instructor at Camp Pendleton. His next transfer brought him to the 5th Marine Division, where he was assigned as executive officer of Company E.[7]

"If You Get to the Top, Put It Up"

Before beginning the climb, which promised to be arduous, Schrier led his men to the 2nd Battalion, 28th Marines, command post for a pep talk from Lieutenant Colonel Johnson. Following the pep talk, as the patrol moved out on its trek into the unknown, Johnson handed a largish folded American flag to George Schrier; the 54-by-48-inch flag[8] had been obtained for Johnson's battalion weeks earlier in Hawaii by the battalion adjutant, Lieutenant Greeley Wells, from the transport USS *Missoula*, which had carried the battalion to Saipan for transfer to the LST that had carried it to Iwo Jima.

Schrier stuffed the folded national colors down the front of his utility blouse. As he turned to lead the patrol up the volcano, Johnson said to him, "If you get to the top, put it up."[9] It was a little after 0800 hours.

During the patrol's brief stay at the battalion forward command post, located at the base of the volcano's eastern slope, several hospital corpsmen, litter bearers drawn from a casual (replacement) battalion attached to the 28th Marines, 12 men from the Company E machine-gun section, and at least three Company E 60mm mortar crewmen had been told off from their own units to join the 3rd Platoon patrol, and a Marine combat photographer asked to be attached to the party,[10] bringing the complement to 44, the size of a full-strength infantry platoon in 1945.

One more man joined the procession as the patrol passed the Company F command post. The importance of the patrol's mission required that Lieutenant Schrier be in constant communication with Lieutenant Colonel Johnson, and so the battalion's portable radio assets had to be rejiggered to provide a radio and a radioman. It fell to Company F to fulfill the need, and the Company F battalion radioman, Private First Class Raymond Jacobs, was selected. According to Jacobs:

> At about the time, while Lieutenant Schrier's patrol moved toward F Company lines, the word was passed that there was a call for me on the company phone at our [command post]. The phone call was an order from Battalion, telling me that a patrol from E Company would soon be passing through F Company lines. I was to turn on my radio, check in with Battalion, and wait for the E Company patrol. When I saw the patrol, I was to report to the

patrol leader and accompany him up Suribachi to provide radio communication between the patrol and Battalion.

When the patrol appeared, I made contact with Lieutenant Schrier and repeated my orders. He told me to fall in and said, "Let's go."[11]

Intent on both moving and exercising his step up from platoon sergeant to platoon leader on February 21, 20-year-old Platoon Sergeant Boots Thomas called out, "Patrol, up the hill. Come on, let's move out."[12]

With that, the patrol stepped over the battalion front line—and Captain Dave Severance had a moment of crystal-clear regret. "I thought I was sending them to their deaths. I thought the Japanese were waiting for them."[13]

The success of the stamina-sapping climb to Suribachi's summit smacks of inevitability now, but at 0800 hours on February 23, 1945, it was a potentially fatal decision to dispatch 45 young men armed with only portable infantry weapons to the steep, shell-blasted side of the volcano when everyone involved knew that the feature was well defended by at least a few hundred well-armed, diehard Japanese troops. There is no explaining the sanguine and sanguinary leap Chandler Johnson was taking with other people's lives, but Johnson had his orders, and he was willing to issue like orders to his troops, who, following months of training and four days of combat under his fiery brand of leadership, trusted him to do right by them.

"Our Colors Are Up!"

Following on several days of bad weather, it was clear, bright day, cool and invigorating with excellent visibility. Perhaps thousands of Marines could follow the patrol's progress all the way up the flank of the volcano.[14]

Just as the Schrier patrol stepped off to climb the volcano, Sergeant Sherman Watson's four-man Company F patrol came into view, heading downslope toward the 2nd Battalion command post.[15]

The Schrier patrol made a rapid, surprisingly uneventful ascent, but in some places, according to radioman Jacobs, the trail was so steep and the ground was so rough that the Americans were forced to crawl on their hands and knees.[16]

Captain Fred Haynes, the 28th Marines assistant operations officer, recalled years later that there was a fire-support plan in place to protect the patrol by boxing it in on three sides with curtains of artillery fire. Haynes had his heart in his mouth as the patrol zigzagged skyward amidst the roar and thunder of the artillery; one misplaced exploding shell could put an end to the gambit. But Schrier's men made such good progress during the climb that they eventually outran the ability of the artillery to safely keep pace. The big guns had to cease firing.[17]

Bradley

Pharmacist's Mate Second Class John Bradley, who was attached to Platoon Sergeant Boots Thomas's 3rd Platoon, Company E, was interviewed by the U.S. Navy's history division in mid-April 1945:

> … the reason we reached the top of Mount Suribachi without a single enemy shot being fired was because the Japs were still in their caves waiting for the bombardment to be lifted. When we reached the top we formed our battle line and we all … [attacked] together, and much to our surprise we didn't find a Jap in sight. If one Jap had been up there manning one of his guns I think he could have pretty well taken care of our 40-man patrol.
>
> Mount Suribachi was a [volcanic] mountain approximately 560 feet high, and … it was hollow on top, with about a … twenty-foot ledge that you could walk all the way around before this crater sank in. This crater was … approximately fifty to sixty feet deep, and it was down in this crater that the Japs were honeycombed in these caves. They had the caves dug in all the way around this crater. Suribachi was inactive at the time, but we noticed smoke, sort of a vapor, coming out of the ground up on this crater, but it was purely inactive …. [18]
>
> Well, the minute we got up on top we set our … [defensive perimeter firing positions] up. [Lieutenant Schrier] placed the machine guns where he wanted them, had our riflemen spotted, and immediately we sent patrols to the right and to the left. We [had gone] up the mountain almost in the middle, so consequently we sent patrols around to the right and left to take care of any Japs that might come out. When we got there, I was with the group that swung to the left and immediately the lieutenant sent a man around to look for a piece of [flagpole] that we could put the American flag on.[19]

The battle-hardened Marines scoured the summit for Japanese who might put up a fight, found no opposition, and then manned defensive positions, facing inward, around the rim of the crater. Bewildered by the utter lack of resistance, several volunteers stood down from the search for the enemy to look for a way to get the flag up.

Private First Class Ray Jacobs was attending to Lieutenant Schrier when he spotted several Marines pulling a piece of pipe from the ubiquitous debris on the ground.

Corporal Robert Leader and Private First Class Leo Rozek were sorting through rubble in a mountaintop cistern when they came across a suitable flagpole in the form of a 7-foot length of iron water pipe, part of the now-demolished freshwater catchment system the Japanese had installed on the volcano. Leader and Rozek carried the heavy pipe to the highest point on the summit[20] and several other Marines, including Lieutenant Schrier, along with Ray Jacobs, closed in to get the flag attached using lengths of cord each member of Company E carried.[21]

Corporal Chuck Lindberg, a flamethrower operator serving as the 3rd Platoon's Assault Squad leader, and Sergeant Hank Hansen, the 3rd Platoon guide, secured the flag to the pole—which was held steady by the Assault Squad's Private Phil Ward—using cord they ran through holes that were probably bombardment damage. When the flag was secured, Lindberg began to scrape a hole in the ground by pounding the heel of his right boondocker against the hard-packed surface. Several Marines sought to enlarge the hole in the ground and provide rocks to hold the flagpole in place, but events outpaced them; Schrier ordered the flag to be raised. Without ceremony, Lieutenant Schrier and four Marines raised the flag upright, and U.S. Navy hospital corpsman John Bradley grabbed the pole in both hands to steady it as the bottom end was driven into the ground. According to radioman Jacobs, "We [took] turns pushing the flagpole deeper, stamping dirt, and jamming rocks round the base of the pipe, trying to secure it. The ground around us [had] been torn up by bombing and shelling. [It was] typical of the terrain on the sides of Suribachi."[22]

Without fanfare or advance notice, the flag was instantly visible to thousands of Americans and Japanese at about 1030 hours.

"Our colors are up … snapping and waving in the breeze."[23]

Hansen

Henry Oliver "Hank" Hansen, the right guide of Company E's 3rd Platoon, was born in Somerville, Massachusetts, on December 14, 1919. He enlisted in the Marine Corps in 1938, fresh out of high school. In 1942, he volunteered for the new parachute training course and was shipped to the Pacific for the invasion of Empress Augusta Bay, Bougainville, in the northern Solomon Islands. When the Marine Corps parachute regiment was disbanded, Sergeant Hank Hansen was reassigned to the 5th Marine Division's Company E, 2nd Battalion, 28th Marines.[24]

Lindberg

Charles W. "Chuck" Lindberg was born on June 26, 1920, in Grand Forks, North Dakota. He enlisted in the Marine Corps shortly after Pearl Harbor was attacked by the Imperial Japanese Navy and volunteered for service with the Marine Raiders the same day he graduated from the boot camp in San Diego. The 2nd Raider Battalion

(Carlson's Raiders) was activated on February 19, 1942, and trained in rural San Diego County before it sailed in the spring of 1942 for more training in Hawaii. While serving with the 2nd Raider Battalion, Lindberg took part in the unit's "Long Patrol" on Guadalcanal in late 1942, then in the late-1943 invasion of Bougainville.[25] When the 1st Marine Raider Regiment and its sub-units were disbanded, Corporal Lindberg was transferred with other Raiders to Company E, 2nd Battalion, 28th Marines, where he asked to be trained as a flamethrower operator because he was "built to carry a 72-pound flamethrower."[26]

Lowery

Louis R. Lowery was born in 1916 in Pittsburgh, Pennsylvania, and grew up in that city. After he graduated from high school, Lowery attended business college and the National School of Photography, then became a staff photographer for the Pittsburgh *Post Dispatch* until he enlisted in the Marine Corps as a combat photographer. Assigned to *Leatherneck* magazine, Sergeant Lowery covered six amphibious combat assaults, including Iwo Jima and Okinawa. It is possible that he holds the record for the most combat assaults by an American serviceman in World War II.[28]

A Missed Opportunity

Staff Sergeant Lou Lowery was a 24-year-old staff photographer for *Leatherneck* magazine on assignment to the 5th Marine Division, a veteran of, so far, five island invasions.[27] He had braved the ascent of Suribachi for this moment. He snapped several photos, but he stopped when he had to swap a fresh roll of film into his camera. With his attention riveted on loading the fresh film, Lowery missed seeing the national colors go up. And he did not have film in his camera even if he had seen the flag go up. *No one* took a photograph of the flag being raised.

Unsung

No one at the time thought to take notes. The matter of getting the flag up for all to see had taken on an urgency too great for administrative niceties. The official list would be drawn up when there was time, then again 71 years in the future. The nameless compilers of the well-after-the-fact 1945 list, as originally drawn, used photographs taken by Staff Sergeant Lou Lowery to guide them. Along the way, what should have been a major moment in Marine Corps history—of the Marine Corps' proudest moment—became riven with errors in the documentation for the names, roles, and fates of the flag-raisers. When the first chronicling process was completed in 1945, the list of flag-raisers looked like this: First Lieutenant Harold "George" Schrier, patrol leader; Platoon Sergeant Ernest "Boots" Thomas, Jr., leader of Company E's 3rd Platoon; Sergeant Henry "Hank" Hansen, 3rd Platoon right guide; Corporal Charles "Chuck" Lindberg, leader of the 3rd Platoon Assault Squad; Private Louis Charlo, a member of Company F and participant in the early-morning four-man Watson patrol to the summit of Suribachi; Private First Class James Michels (often misspelled "Michaels"), a member of the 3rd Platoon Assault Squad; and Pharmacist's Mate Second Class John Bradley, the senior of seven corpsman assigned to Company E.[29]

"We Heard a Roar"

"Just moments after the flag was raised," Ray Jacobs recalled, "we heard a roar from down below on the island."[30]

Thousands of Americans all across the island and offshore fairly swooned as the national colors snapped fully open in the breeze. Many of them had been watching the patrol's ascent for some time.

In addition to loud, cathartic cheering by masses of young men, all manner of large and small vessels that were within sight of the volcano's summit sounded their horns, bells, and whistles. Many onlookers thought that the island's defenses had collapsed, for most earlier American flag-raisings in the Pacific had been mainly associated with final victory. But they also had long marked the seizure of important intermediate objectives, as was the case here. Even so, no one was any less jubilant over the sight of Old Glory snapping in the stiff breeze over Suribachi.

Corporal Chuck Lindberg, who had literally had a hand in raising the flag, had not "thought too much about" the flag-raising itself, but he did mark down the loud and protracted cheers and salutes as "a very inspiring moment up there."[31]

"The celebration," in Ray Jacobs' words, "went on for many minutes. It was a highly emotional, strongly patriotic moment for all of us."[32]

Adding to the luster of the moment—though few observers would have known of it—the first American flag to fly over Suribachi was the first American flag to fly over actual conquered Japanese territory, for Iwo Jima was considered to be a distant but core component of the Japanese Empire.

Among the many who spotted the flag on the volcano's summit were Lieutenant General Holland Smith, the highest-ranking Marine Corps field commander in the Pacific, and Secretary of the Navy James Forrestal, who were just coming ashore for the first time. As soon as Secretary Forrestal saw for himself what all the ruckus was about, he turned to General Smith and uttered these immortal words: "Holland, the raising of that flag on Suribachi means a Marine Corps for the next five hundred years." Moments later, the story goes, Forrestal told Smith that he wanted the flag. The story that Forrestal wanted the flag was soon passed to the 2nd Battalion, 28th Marines, command post, where it caught up with Lieutenant Colonel Chandler Johnson, who blurted out, "To hell with that!"[33] and decided in the moment that the flag was now too valuable to leave on Suribachi, where a superior might grab it as a trophy. Johnson then dispatched his assistant battalion operations officer, Lieutenant Albert "Ted" Tuttle, to scrounge a replacement. As Tuttle left the battalion command post, Johnson shouted an afterthought that he wanted a larger flag than the one already flying on Suribachi.

The Japanese React

Private First Class Ray Jacobs, the Company F radioman on loan to George Schrier, was attending to Schrier's communications needs, standing a few feet from the national colors, when he probably became the first American atop Suribachi to see and experience what can be assumed to have been the Japanese reaction to the flag-raising.

Jacobs was idly eavesdropping on Lieutenant Schrier's end of a radio conversation with Lieutenant Colonel Johnson about the progress of the mission. As Schrier ended the conversation, Jacobs noticed motion below and to his left. He reflexively turned his head to follow the motion and thus spotted a brown-uniformed Imperial Japanese Army soldier as he ran behind a mound of dirt on the crater's lower rim. The Japanese stopped, armed a hand grenade by slapping it against his steel helmet, and threw it overhand toward Jacobs. The grenade fell short and exploded, injuring no one.

Jacobs opened fire. The Japanese soldier withdrew, but many other Japanese broke cover from hidden caves around the crater and threw hand grenades.[34]

Chuck Lindberg spotted a Japanese soldier in a cave entrance about a hundred yards from the flag. Another Marine "nailed" the Japanese, Lindberg doused the cave with his flamethrower, and a Marine demolitions assault man sealed the cave with explosives. (Lindberg noted: "Later we dug [the cave] open and found out there were 73 [dead Japanese] in there."[35]

All hands in the immediate area went on the offensive until no more Japanese or caves could be found in fighting distance of the flag.[36]

When Japanese soldiers imperiled the knot of Marines surrounding the flagpole with gunfire and grenades, the Marines responded with flamethrowers, Browning Automatic Rifles (BARs), and rifle and carbine fire. Ray Jacobs saw individual Marines and Marine fire teams firing as they ran toward the nearest caves.[37]

When a Japanese soldier attacked the *Leatherneck* photographer, Staff Sergeant Lou Lowery, from the mouth of a cave, a Browning Automatic rifleman cut down the intruder, but then a sword-wielding officer leaped into the scene. A Marine shot him dead with a .45-caliber automatic pistol, but then more grenades were hurled from cover. Staff Sergeant Lowery had to drop his camera and leap down the side of the volcano to avoid the bursting grenades, but other Marines opened fire on the caves, and a flamethrower team moved in to douse each one with flaming fuel.

The *Leatherneck* magazine photographer, the only American injured—just scrapes and bruises—in the flare-up of Japanese resistance, climbed back up to the summit to reclaim his camera. It was broken, but the exposed film was salvageable.

Marines peppered several cave mouths with gunfire, and the skirmish near the flag ended while Japanese troops holding other defensive positions farther out made themselves known. The flag snapping in a brisk breeze was all but forgotten.

The Marines near the crater employed flamethrowers and demolitions to reduce opposition from caves on both sides of the rim of the crater. The flickering fight was thus swiftly concluded, Jacobs noted, "with Japanese resistance buried."[38]

Lieutenant Schrier and radioman Jacobs moved from the summit to a less conspicuous position lower down while Schrier's Marines turned to their real work, which was securing the summit and turning it into an observation post. Schrier was able to respond to questions and comments from Lieutenant Colonel Johnson while he controlled the movement of his troops caught up in the clearing operation. When Johnson asked Schrier if it was okay to send up photographers and news writers to cover the flag-raising story, the harried lieutenant agreed.[39]

CHAPTER 5

The Second Flag

Pilgrims

Among those drawn to the volcano's beflagged summit was the Company F commanding officer, Captain Art Naylor, who showed up after the first flag-raising with an unrecorded number of combat troops, apparently including a return by all four members of Sergeant Watson's four-man morning patrol to the summit. Ostensibly, the Company F men were there to help bolster Company E's hold on the best military vantage point on the island, but, just as likely, they had come to gawk, to take part in what was already being touted as an historical moment.[1]

Also drawn to the flag were two who came to do God's work: the 2nd Battalion's navy chaplain, Lieutenant Charles Suver, and his assistant. As soon as the two could set up, Father Suver celebrated Mass.[2]

In addition to a handful of service and civilian news reporters—so far—a Marine still photographer, Private Robert Campbell, joined the trek to the summit of the Suribachi volcano, as did a Marine movie cameraman, Sergeant William Genaust. Another trekker was the myopic 33-year-old Associated Press photographer, Joe Rosenthal, who had already accompanied Marines to Guam and Peleliu and survived four days on Iwo Jima.

Berthed aboard USS *Eldorado*, the invasion fleet flagship, Rosenthal had attempted to get to work early on February 23, but he needed at least an hour to dry off after falling into the sea while transferring to a landing craft. He did reach shore right behind Lieutenant General Holland Smith and Secretary of the Navy James Forrestal, whom he photographed and was photographed with after the first flag went up on Suribachi. Then, though he contrived to not hear the great cacophony of celebration the flag-raising triggered, he took advice from several other correspondents to climb the volcano to see what he could see and photograph anything that looked interesting.[3]

Genaust and Campbell

William Genaust was born on October 12, 1906. He enlisted in the Marine Corps on February 11, 1943, at the age of 36, because he wanted to be a combat cameraman. He was selected to attend the combat camera and still photographer courses offered by the Marine Corps at Quantico, Virginia, and joined the 4th Marine Division photographic section as a sergeant for the invasion of Saipan. He was wounded in the leg on July 9, 1944, when he volunteered to take part in a firefight. Genaust was written up for a Navy Cross, but that request by his commanding officer was downgraded two steps to a Bronze Star, "because he was a cameraman and not an infantryman."[5] Though he was ordered home for a long period of rest and recuperation, Sergeant Genaust honored a request that he volunteer to join the 5th Marine Division photographic section for the invasion of Iwo Jima.[6]

Very little is known about Robert Campbell, which is amazing when one considers his place in this most-historical of Marine Corps moments. We know that he had worked at the *San Francisco Chronicle* and he had volunteered for service in the Marine Corps as a combat photographer. And that's about it.

Rosenthal was gladdened when he ran into Bob Campbell, because the two had known each other from working the San Francisco news beat before leaving for the war. Of even greater importance to Rosenthal was the fact that Marines Campbell and Genaust were armed and civilian Rosenthal was not.[4]

Genaust and Campbell didn't just happen to show up at the 2nd Battalion command post; they had been dispatched by the 5th Marine Division photographic officer, Warrant Officer Norman Hatch, specifically to photograph the replacement of the first flag to fly atop Suribachi. Hatch, who had bravely wielded a movie camera, usually under fire, during the November 1943 invasion of Tarawa, didn't dispatch Genaust and Campbell up to Suribachi's summit on a whim. According to Hatch, "My boss, Lieutenant Colonel George A. Roll [the 5th Marine Division intelligence officer], came to me about 1100 and said that Major General Keller Rockey [the 5th Marine Division commanding general] had requested that a larger flag be flown that could be easily seen by all combat troops. The larger flag was considered to be a morale booster. Lieutenant Colonel Roll advised that I had better get my photographers up on the mountain to photograph the second flag-raising as it would be considered the official flag-raising for the island. Fortunately, Genaust and Campbell were in my command post replenishing their film supplies, so I sent them right away."[7]

(There appear to have been two separate efforts to replace the first flag atop Suribachi. One was forged by Lieutenant Colonel Chandler Johnson for the purpose of safeguarding for his troops a souvenir of their bloody victory from D-day to D+4. The second path was forged by adherence to an order promulgated by Major General Rockey (if not from his superiors) to install a much larger flag on the summit in service of maintaining morale throughout V Amphibious Corps. These two paths happened to reach a confluence at Johnson's forward command post in the late morning of February 23, where photographers Genaust and Campbell arrived at about the same time Lieutenant Tuttle showed up with the larger flag, which appears to have been ordered by Johnson before General Rockey's order went out.)

The pair of Marine photographers joined forces and was about to leave the 2nd Battalion, 28th Marines, command post to begin the ascent when Lieutenant Ted Tuttle of the 2nd Battalion operations staff arrived with a very large flag—96-by-56 inches[8]—under his arm. He had talked the flag out of the possession of a navy ensign aboard *LST 779* as it, the very first LST to do so, disgorged gear on the beach. The ensign had liberated the big flag from a sail locker at Pearl Harbor's Salvage Depot, so he had no idea where it had previously resided. As the means to secure the first flag for the battalion, Lieutenant Colonel Chandler Johnson turned this second flag over to Private First Class René Gagnon, a Company E runner who had already been charged with carrying fresh radio batteries to the summit.

Two squads of Company E's 2nd Platoon had just returned from a patrol around most of Suribachi. Private First Class Ira Hayes later wrote: "[We] had no longer [sic] set down for a rest when word was sent down for our squad leader, Sgt. Strank, from our Captain Severance. Strank left for the company CP & returned a few minutes after & said 4 men were to ascend Suribachi. He then picked [Franklin] Sousley, myself, and Harlon [Block], & also Strank himself. At the time, we didn't know what our mission was, but we were certainly uneasy."[9]

Runner Gagnon joined up with the four 2nd Platoon Marines, who were being dispatched to provide Lieutenant George Schrier with a hard field-telephone link to the battalion command post. The names of the wire party Marines were Sergeant Michael Strank, Corporal Harlon Block, Private First Class Ira Hayes, and Private First Class Franklin Sousley. (Strank was the squad leader and Hayes and Sousley served under fire-team leader and assistant squad leader Block. Hayes was the team automatic rifleman.)

Lieutenant Colonel Johnson told Sergeant Strank to make sure Lieutenant Schrier secured the first flag for the battalion commander and raised the

D-day, February 19, 1945

Eight Square Miles of Hell: An aerial view of Iwo Jima. Suribachi is in the lower right corner. (Official U.S. Army Air Forces photo)

Suribachi under bombardment on February 18, 1945. (Official U.S. Navy photo)

Troop-laden amphibian tractors on their way to the beach. (Official USMC photo)

Troop-laden landing craft on their way to the beach. (Official USMC photo)

The 28th Marines' first waves are about to land on Beach Green. (Official U.S. Navy photo)

Weapons carts powered by Marines are slowed by slippery black ash as infantrymen hurdle the first terrace. (Official USMC photo)

Marines peek over the summit of the final ash terrace, wondering where and when the Japanese will commence firing. Meanwhile, the Marines ashore attempt to overcome the chaos of their landing. (Official USMC photo)

The Marines have landed and the situation is … confusing. (Official USMC photo)

The Japanese open fire across the entire beachhead. (Official USMC photo)

It's H-Hour-plus-3. Marines have attacked through intense Japanese fire and are beginning to successfully engage defensive positions all along the front line. (Official USMC photo)

A Marine flamethrower operator bravely exposes himself to gunfire as he attempts to burn out a Japanese-held pillbox. (Official USMC photo)

Corpsmen treat the wounded in a shell hole that has been turned into an ad hoc beach-side aid station. (Official USMC photo)

A battery of 3rd Battalion, 13th Marines, 105mm howitzers became the first artillery unit to fully establish itself ashore on D-day. It fired its first mission in direct support of the 28th Marines on D-day afternoon. (Official USMC photo)

Assault on Suribachi

February 20, 1945

Suribachi, looking southwest to northeast. (Official U.S. Navy photo)

Throughout Operation Hot Rocks, all manner of weapons—81mm mortars (shown here), medium and heavy machine guns, artillery, antitank guns, rocket trucks, and carrier-based aircraft—supported the 28th Marines assault to surround and reduce the Suribachi defensive complex. (Official USMC photo)

As a carrier-based bomber prepares to drop its bombs on Suribachi, a 37mm antitank guns is being readied to fire on caves and pillboxes in the hope of breaching them in time to help the infantry. (Official USMC photo)

Marine experimental rocket trucks fire sheaves of rockets meant to soften up the Japanese defenses ahead of an infantry attack. (Official USMC photo)

A near miss by a Japanese mortar fired against Marines as they prepare to advance. (Official USMC photo)

Another large shell hole is transformed into a front-line casualty station. (Official USMC photo)

February 21, 1945

A 37mm antitank gun—small but deadly accurate—chips away with unremitting fire at caves and bunkers at the base of Suribachi. (Official USMC photo)

The Japanese fire back. (Official USMC photo)

A Marine checks in with a wounded man. (Official UMC photo)

White smoke rises from a cave complex under assault by Marine flamethrower teams. (Official USMC photo)

A gargantuan blast engulfs a three-tiered bunker tied in with numerous front-line caves and pillboxes. (Official USMC photo)

February 22, 1945

Following a cold rainy spell, Marines clean wet, abrasive volcanic ash from their weapons. (Official USMC photo)

A busy day at the office. A Marine medium machine-gun team supports infantry assaults by pecking away at Japanese emplacements on Suribachi from a static overwatch position. (Official USMC photo)

Marine infantrymen from the 3rd Battalion, 28th Marines and M4 medium tanks from Company C, 5th Tank Battalion, support one another in an advance that ultimately gobbles up two hundred yards of Japanese-held terrain on February 22. (Official USMC photo)

The 3rd Battalion, 13th Marines' entire complement of twelve 105mm howitzers was dedicated solely to the support of Regimental Combat Team 28's drive to surround and reduce the Japanese holding the Suribachi defensive zone. (Official USMC photo)

The 2nd Battalion, 28th Marines' rear command post on February 22. (Official USMC photo)

second one. (The first flag was handed over to Lieutenant Greeley Wells that afternoon and consigned to the battalion safe, which was aboard a battalion headquarters jeep.)[10]

Sergeant Strank's wire team, with Gagnon, struck out rapidly on its own, one of many little knots of men making their way to conduct business or gawk on the summit or along the way.

Gagnon

René Arthur Gagnon was born to a French-Canadian immigrant couple in Manchester, New Hampshire, on March 7, 1926. His parents separated when he was an infant. As a young boy, he worked beside his mother at a shoe factory and as a Western Union bicycle messenger. When he received his Draft notice in early 1943, René requested duty with the Marine Corps Reserve and left home on May 6, bound for the Marine Corps Recruit Depot at Parris Island, South Carolina. He was promoted private first class upon graduation from boot camp on July 16, 1943, and received orders to the Marine Guard Company at the navy yard in Charleston, South Carolina. Eight months later, another transfer took him to the 5th Marine Division's Military Police Company at Camp Pendleton, California. Finally, Gagnon was transferred on April 8, 1944, to the 2nd Battalion, 28th Marines, where he was selected as the Company E battalion runner, working directly for Captain Dave Severance.[11]

Strank

Sergeant Michael Strank—a squad leader in the 2nd Platoon, Company E, 28th Marines—was born on November 10, 1919, in Jarabina, Czechoslovakia. His father left home to find his fortune in America when Mike was a young adult, and it took him three years in a Bethlehem Steel coal mine to save enough cash to buy passage for his family to Franklin Borough, Pennsylvania, near Johnstown. Strank graduated from high school in June 1937, joined the Civilian Conservation Corps for 18 months, and then worked as a laborer for the Pennsylvania state highway department. He joined the Marine Corps on October 6, 1939, on a four-year enlistment. (Apparently no one involved in recruiting or processing Strank noticed that he remained a Czechoslovakian citizen of Slovak descent—quite possibly an "enemy alien!"—throughout his time in the Marine Corps.)[12] He graduated boot camp at Parris Island, South Carolina, in December 1939, and served in various capacities at Parris Island until reassigned to Guantanamo Bay, Cuba, in January

1941. He subsequently bounced around the East Coast and was promoted corporal in April 1941. He was stationed at New River, North Carolina, with the 1st Marine Division when Pearl Harbor was attacked, and was promoted sergeant in January 1942. He sailed to Samoa with a Marine infantry battalion and landed on Uvea in May. He next served with the independent 22nd Marine Regiment and was transferred to the 3rd Marine Raider Battalion, with which he took part in the bloodless seizure of Pavuvu in the Russell Islands. In November 1943, Sergeant Strank experienced first combat at Empress Augusta Bay, Bougainville, in the northern Solomon Islands. When Marine Raider units were disbanded in February 1944, Strank was shipped to San Diego and given home leave. Following duty in San Diego, Mike Strank was transferred to Company E and assigned as a squad leader in the 2nd Platoon. When the platoon sergeant's billet opened up during the journey to Iwo Jima, Captain Severance immediately offered it to Strank, but the sergeant declined the honor; he wanted to lead the squad he had trained in combat.[13]

Sousley

Franklin Runyon Sousley was born in Hill Top, Kentucky, on September 19, 1925. He attended a two-room grammar school and ultimately graduated high school in May 1943. An older brother died from complications connected to appendicitis when Franklin was five, and his father died in 1934 at age 35 from diabetes-related complications, leaving nine-year-old Franklin as the male role model for his year-old brother. Following high-school graduation, Franklin moved to Dayton, Ohio, to work in a refrigerator factory. When, in late 1943, he received his Draft notice, Sousley enlisted in the Marine Corps. Upon graduation from boot camp at San Diego, Sousley was assigned to Company E, 2nd Battalion, 28th Marines.[14]

Hayes

Ira Hamilton Hayes, an automatic rifleman serving with the 2nd Platoon, Company E, 28th Marines, was a Pima Indian born on January 12, 1923, in Sacaton, Arizona, a small village in Pinal County's Gila River Indian Community. He was the oldest of six children. His father, a World War I veteran, worked as a subsistence farmer and cotton harvester. Growing up, Ira took after his father, a quiet man, but the son was shyer and more sensitive. He was also known for his English-language skills and an unsurpassed love of books. Hayes completed two years of high school, worked as a carpenter for the Civilian Conservation Corps in May and June 1942, and enlisted in the Marine Corps Reserve on August 26, 1942. As soon as he completed boot camp in San Diego, he volunteered for parachute training. He joined the 3rd

Marine Parachute Battalion on December 2, 1942, which in March 1943 sailed to the South Pacific Area, where it trained and undertook occupation duty. First combat occurred on December 4, 1943, when the 3rd Parachute Battalion entered the fight for Bougainville. By then, Hayes was a private first class and a Browning Automatic rifleman. When the 1st Parachute Regiment and its components were deactivated in February 1944, Hayes and many other paramarines were transferred to the newly authorized 5th Marine Division. In fact, part of Hayes's paramarine company was transferred as a group to Company E, 2nd Battalion, 28th Marines.[15]

The Money Shot

About halfway up the volcano, the 2nd Platoon wire party and Private First Class Gagnon passed Staff Sergeant Lou Lowery, the *Leatherneck* photographer, who was heading downslope to try to find a new camera. Farther down, Lowery stopped to speak to Genaust, Campbell, and Rosenthal, who stopped to exchange news and views as well as to allow Rosenthal to catch his breath. Though Lowery had missed the flag-raising at the summit because he had had his head down while loading film into his camera, he lamented that the ascending photographers had missed the money shot—the flag being raised. None of these men knew about the dispatch of a second flag. When Genaust and Campbell expressed thoughts about turning back, Lowery affirmed, "But you might like to go up. It's a hell of a good view up there."[16] Joe Rosenthal had also been wavering, but Lowery's words somehow left him with renewed interest in completing the rigorous climb to the summit.[17] The climb became even more arduous, especially for the diminutive Rosenthal, who was lugging a very heavy pack.

Ira Hayes describes the wire party's final push to the summit:

> We got 3 quarters of the way up when we stopped for a rest. Then Strank told us we were to go up to the top and raise a large flag so the Marines fighting on the northern side would know we had finally secured Suribachi. A very small flag had been raised about a half-hour before we [arrived].
>
> We got to the top. Strank told Sousley and myself to hunt for something to tie the flag onto. In the meantime Block & Strank was preparing a place to put Old Glory up. By the faith of God we found a pipe just the right length.[18]

Rosenthal later reported:

> The fall of this … fortress in four days of gallant Marine fighting was a great thing. A good story and we should have good pictures.

So in I went, back to more of that slogging thru the deep volcanic ash, warily sidestepping the numerous Japanese mines. Marine [Private] Bob Campbell, a San Francisco buddy of mine, and [Sergeant Bill Genaust] … were with me …

There was an occasional sharp crack of rifle fire close by and the mountainside had a porcupine appearance of bristling all over, what with machine and antiaircraft guns peering from the dugouts, foxholes and caves. There were few signs of life from these enemy spots, however. Our men were systematically blowing out these places and we had to be on our toes to keep clear of our own demolition squads.

As the trail became steeper, our panting progress slowed to a few yards at a time. I began to wonder and hope that this was worth the effort, when suddenly over the brow of the topmost ridge we could spy men working with the flagpole …[19]

The Photo

When the photographers reached the summit, Rosenthal was especially winded. The first thing he saw was the smaller flag, waving in the wind. He walked over to the flag in time for Bob Campbell to photograph him with Bill Genaust and a photographer from *Yank* magazine who had also just arrived. Rosenthal's pose shows him as ebullient.

Hayes: "We gathered around the [second] flagpole, Block at the base to guide the pole into a bunch of rocks him and Strank had fixed up."[20]

The small hubbub from the direction of the larger flag alerted Rosenthal and the others that something of note might be about to take place. As well, other Marines seemed to be getting ready to lower the smaller flag.

Rosenthal thought he might be able to photograph both flags at once, but he was out of position for that and thought—correctly—that he had only seconds to make a move. He decided to shoot the second, larger, flag as it was being raised.[21]

The new flag, which was four times the size of the first, was lashed to another, longer, iron pipe than the first. (The pole, another cistern system artifact pulled out of the rubble of a radar station near the volcano's summit, was scavenged by Hayes and Sousley on an order from Mike Strank.)[22]

As this was going on, in a twinkling, Rosenthal moved to the back wall of the crater, placed his camera on the ground,[23] and frantically piled up some large flat stones and a sandbag to stand on; he was 5-foot-5 and needed the advantage. The shot Rosenthal had composed in his head would provide plenty of room for photographing the entire flag and all the flag-raisers.

While Rosenthal was occupied with getting set to take the shot of the flag going up, Campbell was outside the crater and a few feet downhill, poised to photograph both flags at once. Genaust stood three feet to Rosenthal's left and was a little lower at eye level. His movie camera was loaded with color film—the end of a pre-loaded film cassette was getting close—and Rosenthal shot black-and-white Agfa film.

"I'm not in your way, am I, Joe?" Genaust called out to the nearby still photographer.

"No, it's all right," Rosenthal answered.[24]

The final adjustment to the flag and its pole found Sergeant Strank calling a pair of rubberneckers—Private First Class René Gagnon and an unknown man, later thought to be Pharmacist's Mate John Bradley—over to share the load of lofting the dead weight of the heavy iron pipe and the large wind-controlled flag.[25] Gagnon ended up on the side away from Rosenthal's and Genaust's cameras, and the unknown man ended up on the near side.

Without any warning or preamble, a rather gruff and distracted George Schrier ordered both flags into motion—the first flag down and the second flag up.

Hayes: "Block hollered something, then we heaved all at once. It all happened so quick."[26]

When someone warned, "There she goes," Rosenthal, who was working on pure instinct, turned with his bulky 4×5 Speed Graphic camera at the ready. (For photography buffs: lens setting between f8 and f11; shutter speed at 1/400th second).

Years after the flag-raising, Rosenthal wrote: "Out of the corner of my eye, I had seen the men start the flag up. I swung my camera and shot the scene. That is how the picture was taken, and when you take a picture like that, you don't come away saying you got a great shot."[27]

Rosenthal took one photo as the flag went up. He felt it was a bad shot, because the stones beneath his feet did not offer a solid base.[28]

As Rosenthal got his shot, Bill Genaust exposed 198 frames of 16mm ASA 8 Kodachrome film with his modern Bell & Howell movie camera before the film in its pre-loaded cassette ran out.[29]

The first flag was lowered as the new one rose, and Bob Campbell captured that moment on film. In fact, he took the only photo of both flags at one time, one going up and the other coming down.

The flag switch was so perfectly choreographed that it was easy to think it was the product of some staff officer's anal impulse. But it was a completely rational act made at the behest of Lieutenant George Schrier upon his realization that many battle-rattled Marines across the island had taken to reassuring themselves that their side was winning by taking frequent glances at the flag. If it wasn't there to be seen, Marines might think the Japanese had retaken the heights and morale might plummet. Schrier was so engrossed in making the timing come off for getting the first flag down that he neglected to glance over to see the second flag rise.

Lieutenant Barber Conable, who would become the president of the World Bank, woke up from an exhausted nap to see the second flag flying above Suribachi. He recalled: "It was my first time in battle and we were all terrified. Someone jumped into my foxhole and swore: 'It wasn't like this on Bougainville.' … When she heard about [the flag-raising], Tokyo Rose said the flag on the mountain would be thrown into the sea. I hadn't had any sleep for more than 60 hours, so I didn't see them raise it, and it was wonderful to wake up to. I must say I got a little weepy when I saw it."[30]

As with the first flag, no one took note of who actually raised the second flag. No one jotted down the names. Only the flag-raisers themselves might have known who some of the others were, but none of the flag-raisers appear to have known the identities of all six, or even that there were as many as six—and only six—touching the improvised flagpole when it was heaved toward the sky.

As soon as the new flag went up, three Marines pushed the foot of the pole deeper into the pile of shell-blasted volcanic rubble. Rosenthal shot that moment, too, but also discounted it right away.

Hayes: "[A] Marine at the side hollered over to us & said if we knew our pictures were taken."[31]

Then, as lines were deployed to steady the large flag on the windy summit, sixteen Marines and two navy medical corpsmen rushed around the flagpole to get into a triumphal "class photo" arranged by Rosenthal. In what came to be called the "Gung Ho" shot, these Marines and corpsmen raised their weapons or headgear at Rosenthal's enthusiastic urging and cheered on cue from the energized photographer. Rosenthal, still on his wobbly perch, took a shot of them while Campbell took a shot of Rosenthal taking the Gung Ho shot. Rosenthal took an insurance shot, too, because he felt in his bones that only the Gung Ho view was worth the arduous climb up Suribachi's northern flank; they clearly demonstrated a moment of authentic if directed triumph in a new island invasion that, so far, hardly seemed triumphal.[32]

Then the moment passed. Rosenthal had taken just four photos of the second flag: one going up, one of Marines securing it, the Gung Ho shot, and a back-up of the Gung Ho shot. (He took 18 photos in all on February 23, most of them pro forma and utterly forgettable.)[33] Campbell had taken more photos than Rosenthal atop Suribachi, and Genaust was on his way to exposing several hundred feet of color movie film.

Hayes: "We [posed for the group photos] then quickly shoved on back down the volcano to our company."[34]

Joe Rosenthal described the immediate aftermath: "I tried to find the four men I heard were the actual instigators of the grand adventure. But they had scattered to their units and I finally gave it up and descended the mountain to get the pictures out and on their way to possible publication."[35]

The raising of the second flag evoked no spontaneous cheers, no celebratory horns, no keening whistles, no special attention. All anyone near Suribachi's summit could hear was the nearby sound of men's voices, the incessant wind, and the clatter and bang of distant battle. The event went largely unnoticed and unremarked by V Amphibious Corps and Japanese adversaries locked in stubborn battle down below.

It was getting crowded atop Suribachi. Pretty soon, the blasted moon-like landscape was filled with people—soldierly and unsoldierly—carrying cameras and notepads. Marines who weren't occupied in keeping an eye out for a Japanese attack were submitting to interviews and photo opportunities.

Another visitor was Lieutenant Keith Wells, who had led Company E's 3d Platoon until he had been painfully wounded on the approaches to Suribachi on February 21. After turning his command over to Platoon Sergeant Boots Thomas and submitting to medical treatment aboard the hospital ship USS *Samaritan*, Wells, who was well respected as a hard charger, went absent from the ship and roped several Marines who had come down to report the morning's events to the 2nd Battalion, 28th Marines, command post into going back. He then limped—with assistance—to the summit to spend some time with his men.

CHAPTER 6

Cropping History

In Search of a Hero

In the late afternoon of February 23, Platoon Sergeant Boots Thomas, whose 3rd Platoon of Company E was still detailed to hold the perimeter atop Suribachi, was ordered by Lieutenant George Schrier to report long before sunrise the next morning aboard the invasion fleet flagship, USS *Eldorado*, to discuss the flag-raising.[1]

Thomas most likely did not know that he was going in place of Schrier, who had the impression that the Marine Corps and Department of the Navy were looking for someone to play all-around hero in the publicity wars of the day. Ever the strong, silent type who got things done without fanfare or self-aggrandizement, Schrier evaded the tacitly proffered notoriety by tacitly proffering Platoon Sergeant Thomas to be the focal point of flag-raising publicity (because, until Joe Rosenthal's second-flag-raising photo moved on the Associated Press wire, the first flag was *the* Pacific War story from which headlines would be made).

Interviewing Thomas as soon as he came aboard the *Eldorado* were Vice Admiral Richmond Kelly Turner, the Fifth Fleet transport chief, and Lieutenant General Holland Smith, the Pacific Theater's highest-ranking Marine.[2]

Thomas was next turned over aboard the flagship to CBS radio correspondent Don Pryor. The live broadcast began at 0430 Iwo Jima time in order that it reach U.S. East Coast listeners at 2.30 p. m. Eastern War Time.[3]

In his introduction, Pryor asserted that Thomas was "the first American in history who has ever raised Old Glory over a part of the Japanese empire." This was followed by a moment of dead air while Thomas gathered his thoughts. Then, "No, Mr. Pryor, I don't want to give that impression. The honor belongs to every man in the platoon. Three of us actually raised the flag: Lieutenant Harold G. Schrier, our company executive officer; Sergeant H. O. Hansen of Boston; and myself. But the rest of the men had just as big a part in it as we did."[4]

Admitting that he was "mighty proud," Thomas went on to share even more credit by specifically identifying two members of his platoon as "the first men to reach the spot where the flag was raised," the first man to shoot a Japanese soldier, and even Company F Marines who had occupied defensive positions on the crater's southern rim.[5]

Don Pryor was doing his best to cast Thomas in the role of prime hero on Suribachi, but Thomas kept diverting the praise to others. Frustrated at every turn, the veteran journalist finally gave up and turned the young platoon sergeant loose to get some needed sleep aboard ship. Parting ways with "I think you've done your share for a few hours" when he signed off, Pryor reminded his listeners that they had just heard from the man who had *led* the assault up Suribachi, a refutation of Thomas's modest claims for his role in the flag-raising.[6]

Before getting his peaceful nap, Boots posed for photos on the flagship's bridge with General Smith, who treated the 20-year-old Floridian to several of his iconic cigars.[7]

What Thomas did not know but George Schrier strongly suspected was that the heady call aboard the *Eldorado* was an audition for the Marine who would be billed as America's next great war hero. By acting naturally, just like himself, Boots Thomas was adjudged ready to meet the challenge. He was photogenic, he was fearless, he was well-spoken and intelligent, he was young but had practical wisdom. If anything, Boots Thomas was too direct, too honest, too modest. Perhaps fame would cure him of these faults.

Boots Thomas's CBS interview appeared to drive a stake through the heart of Technical Sergeant Keyes Beech's plan to make a hero out of Thomas. Beech, a well-known foreign correspondent and feature writer before he volunteered for the Marine Corps, was on temporary assignment with the 5th Marine Division public information team when he was handed the job of turning Thomas into the Marine hero of the moment. Listening to the Pryor interview on CBS convinced Beech that a tough job lay ahead just in the preliminary task of convincing Thomas that he was the hero he claimed he wasn't. Following is a clever example of Beech's effort to mix several unconnected story lines into a narrative news report that suggested—but did not overtly claim—that Thomas was indeed the hero Beech was ordered to claim he was. Only roughly half of the piece is really about Thomas or his 3rd Platoon troops, and the exciting action that it depicts appears to be more about Boots Thomas's February 21

Navy Cross action than the brief February 23 firefight that broke out right after the first flag was raised.[8] This and several variations were dispatched to scores, if not hundreds, of news outlets and would appear in print or be heard from the air waves for several months.

Hottest Flag Raising
TSgt Keyes Beech
Marine Combat Correspondent
Leatherneck, May 1945
The raising of the Stars and Stripes on the crest of Mount Suribachi on Iwo Jima was one of the hottest flag raising ever staged anywhere. Even as Marine Platoon Sergeant Ernest I. Thomas, 20, of Tallahassee, Fla., and his men began set up the flag pole a Jap popped out of a cave to hurl a grenade at them.

Other grenades followed, and Thomas and his men went after the Japs while two Marines stayed behind to protect the flag. The flag raising continued after the grenade-throwing Japs had been cleaned out.

And in the four-day battle that ended when the flag was planted on Mount Suribachi, these things happened:

A lone Marine charged an enemy pillbox and was met by a saber-swinging Jap Lieutenant. The Marine grabbed the sword with his bare hands, took it away from the Jap and cut off his head.

Two companies of Marines engaged in a grenade-throwing contest with the Japs, not daring to use rifles for fear of hitting their own men. When daylight came they counted 77 dead Japs in the area.

One Marine took 10 Japs with him in death. Alone, he stormed a pillbox and killed the 10 before he himself was slain.

Two squads of Marines were isolated by enemy fire at the base of Suribachi 200 yards ahead of their lines. Two of the Marines were killed, eight wounded. The rest fought their way back in darkness, dragging the eight wounded with them.

The Jap mortars are good, but so are ours. So good, in fact, that one night a Jap ran up to a Marine mortar emplacement and shouted, "Cease firing!"

Marine demolition crews planted a 180-pound charge in a cave at the foot of Suribachi. A Jap picked it up and set it outside the cave, then turned around and started back. The Marines shot him and put the charge back where it belonged.

A Jap scrambled out of a pillbox and took off with a Marine hot on his heels, jabbing a bayonet at his rear. But another Marine cut down the Jap with a Browning automatic rifle.

Sergeant Edward D. Jones, 30, of Stanwood, Wash., spoke enough Japanese to urge a wounded Jap to come out of a pillbox. The Jap refused, until Jones threatened to turn a flame thrower on the pillbox. The Jap, second prisoner to be taken on the island, told Jones his father operates a grocery store in Hawaii.

First Lieutenant Harold H. Stirling, 23, of Drexel Hill, and his platoon met a dawn attack by 40 or 50 Japs. Just minutes later the platoon had wiped out all of them with a loss of two Marines killed and several wounded.

"I guess you could say we caught hell," said soft-spoken Platoon Sergeant Thomas, who led the group of Marines raising the national colors over Suribachi.

"In my platoon we lost 17 men out of 46, in about 45 minutes at one time. That was when our platoon leader was wounded; I had to take over.

"After that," continued Thomas, "I don't remember much. I think I led some tanks to fire into pillboxes and caves.

"I remember a Jap coming out of a pillbox and setting up a Nambu [light machine gun] on top of it. I think about 50 of us shot at him at once.

"Another thing I remember was a Marine climbing up on a pillbox with a demolition charge. A Jap came out of the pillbox—he didn't know the Marine was there—and started to run away. The Marine leaped on his back and killed him with a knife."[9]

The flurry of activity around efforts to raise Boots Thomas in the public consciousness took place in a tiny wedge of time before the first flag and the first-flag-raisers were crowded out of view by the serendipitous artistry of the second-flag photograph taken by Joe Rosenthal.

Events outran the news cycle.

Cropping History

Joe Rosenthal turned his undeveloped film over to a public information officer aboard the *Eldorado* during the late afternoon of February 23, and it was dispatched aboard a U.S. Navy courier seaplane to Guam via a regularly scheduled press run. (Film shot by Lou Lowery and Bob Campbell apparently went out by mail and it appears that none of it was developed until it reached the United States.[10] Bill Genaust's movie film was held for hand-delivery to U.S.-based documentary filmmakers in mid-March.)[11]

Rosenthal was not especially impressed with what he believed were the mediocre results of his day's exertions. As far as the photographer was concerned, he had missed *the* historic moment of the Iwo Jima campaign when the first flag went up, had huffed and puffed up the fierce mountain to photograph an irrelevant substitution, and had pretty much botched the shot over a question of firm footing.

Unbeknownst to Rosenthal until he saw his flag-raising photo in print—days later—a photo editor on Guam cropped the original horizontal photo into a dramatic vertical image by eliding a lot of background noise and focusing tightly on a solid artistic pyramid of Marines beneath the rising national colors. What in the photographer's own mind felt like an ordinary, rather pedestrian shot of little value had been turned into *The Photo*, an unsurpassed and unsurpassable masterpiece—immortal, emotional, fervent. The ultimate expression of American patriotism.[12]

Acclaim and Controversy

The Rosenthal photos went from the photo technicians on Guam to the Guam office of the Associated Press, Rosenthal's employer. AP photographic editor John Bodkin was immediately struck by the flag-raising photo's near perfection. He exclaimed when he saw it, "Here's one for all time!" Bodkin straightaway transmitted the image via radiofax machine directly to the AP headquarters in New York City at about 7 a. m., Eastern War Time. Newspapers throughout the world were grabbing it off the news wire within a scorching seventeen and a half hours of its having been taken. All this occurred before the photographer had an opportunity to take a look for himself.[13]

Among many other consequences—some good, some not so good—the general release of The Photo ruined any chance of further promotion of Boots Thomas as the hero of the moment. Technical Sergeant Keyes Beech's brief public relations campaign, barely begun, took some time—months—to run its course, but in the end, Thomas and the other first-flag-raisers—and the first flag-raising itself—were consigned to obscurity.

Another consequence of the sudden release of Joe Rosenthal's flag-raising photo was—for better or worse—the drowning out of other news from the front lines of Iwo Jima—the masking of total war on the main body of the island. Readers in the United States were lulled—even misled—into believing for a time that the Japanese holding the island were pushovers.[14]

Before he actually saw any of his Suribachi photos, Joe Rosenthal strongly preferred the Gung Ho photo, but all that third flag-raising photo became worth to him was a blight on his professional reputation. It was the one photo of 18 he took on February 23 that he thought was going to be even a modest winner.

A week or so after the flag-raising photo was released to the whole world—except Iwo Jima, it seemed—Rosenthal himself flew to Guam and was almost immediately asked by a colleague if "the photo" was staged. He had not yet seen his Suribachi photos in their final form, or even as test prints. He thought the question was about the photo he had staged in the shadow of the second flag, the Gung Ho photo he preferred, so he replied enthusiastically in the affirmative.

A casual eavesdropper who heard the admission thought the conversation was about the flag-raising shot, the first Rosenthal took atop Suribachi.

It took a few minutes for Rosenthal to realize that he had made a big mistake, and too much time had passed to take it all back. The result was many accusations over the rest of his long life that the *flag-raising* photo had been staged. This made very little difference to the masses of Americans—of multiple generations—who loved and still love the flag-raising photo, but petty professional jealousies plagued Rosenthal's reputation while he was alive and are still in circulation today.[15]

One of Rosenthal's leading detractors with respect to the "staged" photo rumor was Lou Lowery. This 24-year-old Marine's frustration at missing out on the glory is understandable, but it is difficult to understand the enmity with which the anti-Rosenthal campaign was taken up by the casual eavesdropper himself: Robert Sherrod, a courageous and highly respected war correspondent working for *Time* and *Life* magazines. Sherrod, who bore no obvious enmity toward Joe Rosenthal, eventually admitted to being responsible for spreading the rumor, and he later apologized and admitted that he was wrong. Lowery also apologized and, in due course, became a good friend of Rosenthal's.[16]

Simply watching the 198 frames of Bill Genaust's second-flag-raising film, once it became widely available, would have immediately dispelled this disheartening nonsense.

A Superb Photo

How could anyone know that the visual product of Joe Rosenthal's unbalanced stance and rushed demeanor were bound for glory? The photographer himself felt that he had failed to take a competent—much less superb—photograph of the second flag's arc across the smoke-marred heavens.

Other photos of other Marine Corps flag-raisings on other Pacific islands are pretty much pro forma: typically, senior officers—sometimes a general—are present; there's at least a semblance of a color guard and at least a hint of military decorum. All planned, all bland.

Both Suribachi flag-raisings were unique. One junior officer was present on the summit for both of them, Lieutenant George Schrier. No one more senior than Schrier attended the raising of the first flag, no one more senior than Schrier directed the ad hoc protocol.

The Rosenthal second flag-raising photo in particular is kinetic—bursting with energy. At one end of the scrum is a helmeted Marine piercing the earth with the lower end of the improvised flagpole. At the other end is a Marine who can be seen reaching for the heavens. In between, four American servicemen struggle with a heavy lift while striding purposefully forward. These are activities Marines accomplish all the time, literally and figuratively. Supplementing the still photo is several seconds of moving pictures—not so famous, not often seen, but adding even more action to underscore The Photo's powerful kinetic draw. The other flag—the first flag—was not photographed at all as it rose from the ground to cross the heavens.

CHAPTER 7

Grinding Forward

Clearing Suribachi

Even as the drama atop Suribachi unfolded across the morning and early afternoon of February 23, elements of the 28th Marines along the line at the volcano's base took measures to ensure the security of the enterprise by bringing resistance in southwestern Iwo to an end. The main task was bunker-hunting followed by bunker-busting. Squads and platoons ventured forward to close the noose at the base entirely and advanced up the steep flanks to kill Japanese or seal them permanently into their demolished fortifications. Elements of Company C, 5th Tank Battalion, continued to support the 28th Marines; elements of the 5th Engineer Battalion took control of the demolitions task; and the 12 105mm howitzers of the 3rd Battalion, 13th Marines, and at least several U.S. Navy warships were always on call, ready at a moment's notice to comply with fire-support requests.

For the most part, the Japanese went meekly to their deaths. Perhaps the knowledge that they had been abandoned to their fate, coupled with the mind-erasing effects of incessant and accurate heavy bombardment, not to mention their losing a spectacular battle so spectacularly, brought on this strange collective passivity. This is not to say that they all died quietly; many put up a fight, and American casualties rose.

Nightfall on February 23 found George Schrier's Company E patrol more or less on its own. Most of the "visiting firemen" had departed, and no one sent more reinforcements. There is no record of who was on the summit that night, but it appears that at least 50 armed Americans from Company E and Company F remained in control up there. They spread out and dug in, but the Japanese in bunkers all around them paid scant attention and mounted no assaults. Farther down, an estimated 120 Japanese moved out as individuals or in small groups, left cover, and attempted to flee northward. A few made it all the way to friendly lines—where they were lambasted and humiliated as quitters and threatened with execution—but most died in feeble counterattacks or alone in the dark as they blundered into wary, wide-awake Marines. An organized attempt by 30 Japanese to overrun the 1st Battalion, 28th Marines, command post failed miserably.

It was more of the same after sunrise on February 24; the reinforced 28th Marines continued to hunt down surviving defenders and blow up their caves and hiding holes. A few dazed survivors were captured, but most of the defenders died, many by their own hands. Hundreds were buried beneath the rubble or in little air pockets sealed all around, uncounted and uncountable.

In the end, the 5th Engineer Battalion certified the destruction of 165 concrete pillboxes and bunkers on Suribachi, the sealing of more than 200 caves, and the detonation of thousands of artillery rounds, mines, grenades, and other explosive devices left behind by the dead or fleeing defenders. While an accurate count was made impossible by the willful sealing of hundreds of living Japanese into caves and fighting emplacements, 1,231 Japanese corpses were counted on Suribachi alone.

When it was as over as it needed to be, the 28th Marines was placed in the 5th Marine Division reserve to rest, draw fresh gear, take in replacements, and guard Suribachi. To the north, the rest of V Amphibious Corps had been grinding forward from the beaches to secure post-D-day objectives. The end of the battle for Iwo Jima was nowhere in sight.

Suribachi turned out to be the easy objective. What made it worthwhile when set in contrast to the bloody slog that emblemized the capture of Iwo Jima's three airfields and cleaning out the rest of the island was the advantage in direct observation garnered by its capture. What made it historically significant was The Photo.

March

For a week after the flags were raised, the 5th Marine Division's 28th Marines was the V Amphibious Corps reserve. The regiment pretty much sat on the now-hallowed ground on Suribachi and pulled itself together as an efficient combat unit while the other infantry regiments—including two fresh, veteran regimental combat teams from the 3rd Marine Division—got pulled into a grinding, potentially demoralizing battle of attrition with carefully emplaced Japanese infantry holding the northern portions of the embattled island.

The 28th Marines was alerted on February 28: it would rejoin the action on March 1. The regimental and battalion staffs and company commanders were told that Marines now held about two-thirds of the land area of Iwo Jima and that the 28th Marines would be relieving the 5th Division's 27th Marines in place. When the relief was completed, the 28th was tasked with closing a gap between itself (on the 5th Marine Division's right flank) and the 3rd Marine Division's adjacent left-flank regiment. Japanese defenses on Hill 362-A, facing the 28th Marines, were dense and manned by troops known to be eager to die if that's what it took to kill American Marines. The terrain was rough—a wasteland of myriad twisted gullies and hillocks that had to be engaged head-on.

The 28th Marines' March 1 attack commenced on schedule. Among the Marines at the fore of the attack was flamethrower operator and first-flag-raiser Corporal Chuck Lindberg, leader of the Assault Squad of Company E's 3rd Platoon. Within a very short time of the start of the 28th Marines' attack, Lindberg was culled while evading a friendly flame tank; he was struck by a bullet that passed through his forearm and lodged in the part of his utility blouse that covered his chest. Lindberg was evacuated from the fight, never to return.[1]

Early on, Company E became heavily engaged with Japanese defenders. Sergeant Mike Strank's squad of the 2nd Platoon was pinned down in bewildering terrain for four hours by blistering fire. Finally, Strank called a temporary halt so the squad could dispatch a runner to tell the main body of Company E where it was pinned. Strank then kneeled behind cover to draw a map in the sand. Several members of the squad gathered around him to hear what the plan would be. As the huddle formed, a high-explosive round detonated very close to the Marines. When the smoke cleared, a few of the less-dazed survivors saw that Strank was on his back with his arms over his head and a large hole in his chest. He had been killed instantly by what was probably a 5-inch round fired by a friendly destroyer whose gunners no doubt thought they had a clear—and rare—shot at Japanese troops in the open.[2] Mike Strank was interred in the 5th Marine Division Cemetery on Iwo Jima, then moved to Arlington National Cemetery in 1949. He was the first flag-raiser to die.[3]

Corporal Harlon Block took over leadership of Strank's reeling squad, but he was killed by a Japanese mortar round only a few hours later. His last words were, "They killed me." He was interred in the 5th Marine Division Cemetery, then reinterred in his hometown—Weslaco, Texas—in 1949, then moved a final time to the Marine Military Academy cemetery in Harlingen, Texas.[4]

Also on March 1, Company E's 3rd Platoon lost Sergeant Hank Hansen. The platoon was advancing through twisted terrain when the usual banter Marines tend to enjoy caused Hansen to lose his situational awareness. He was delivering a cutting remark when he inadvertently stepped into the open from behind a little piece of cover. A Japanese machine-gunner immediately shot him dead.[5] He was interred in the 5th Marine Division Cemetery and eventually reinterred in Oahu's National Memorial Cemetery of the Pacific.[6]

Captain Dave E. Severance, USMCR
    Silver Star Citation:
    The President of the United States of America takes pleasure in presenting the Silver Star to Captain Dave E. Severance (MCSN: 0-11101), United States Marine Corps Reserve, for conspicuous gallantry and intrepidity as Commanding Officer of Company E, Twenty-eighth Marines, FIFTH Marine Division, in action against enemy Japanese forces on Iwo Jima, Volcano Islands, on 1 March 1945. When his company was ordered to launch an attack on a heavily defended ridge south of Nishi Village, Captain Severance skillfully directed the assault against this strong enemy position despite stubborn resistance and courageously led his unit in the accomplishment of its mission. Once the objective was gained, he tenaciously held the position which formed a salient in the line. When the enemy made a fanatic effort to dislodge the company with a concentrated barrage of mortar, machine gun and rifle fire, Captain Severance marshaled his men and held the ridge until the friendly units on his flanks were able to advance and regain contact along the entire front. His indomitable fighting spirit, exemplary leadership and courageous devotion to duty were in keeping with the highest traditions of the United States Naval Service.

President Franklin Roosevelt addressed a joint session of the Congress on March 1 (United States time; March 2 Iwo Jima time) to discuss his recent meeting in Yalta (Soviet Union) with the top Allied leaders to lay out a plan for post-war action. During the prepared speech, the President went off the script to issue a warning to the government of Japan:

The Japanese war lords know that they are not being over looked. They have felt the force of our B-29's, and our carrier planes; they have felt the naval might of the United States, and do not appear very anxious to come out and try it again.

The Japs now know what it means to hear that "The United States Marines have landed." And I think I can add that, having Iwo Jima in mind, "The situation is well in hand."

They also know what is in store for the homeland of Japan now that General [Douglas] MacArthur has completed his magnificent march back to Manila and now that Admiral [Chester] Nimitz is establishing air bases right in the back yard of Japan itself—in Iwo Jima.

But, lest somebody else start to stop work in the United States, I repeat what I have so often said—in one short sentence—even in my sleep: "We haven't won the wars yet"—with an s on "wars."

It is still a long, tough road to Tokyo. It is longer to go to Tokyo than it is to Berlin, in every sense of the word. The defeat of Germany will not mean the end of the war against Japan. On the contrary, we must be prepared for a long and costly struggle in the Pacific.

But the unconditional surrender of Japan is as essential as the defeat of Germany. I say that advisedly, with the thought in mind that that is especially true if our plans for world peace are to succeed. For Japanese militarism must be wiped out as thoroughly as German militarism.[7]

Private Louis Charlo was a member of the Bitteroot Salish (or Flathead) tribe. He was born on September 26, 1926, in Missoula, Montana, enlisted in the Marine Corps in 1944, and served as an automatic rifleman with Company F, 28th Marines. Charlo was one of four members of Company F's Watson patrol when it climbed to the summit of Mount Suribachi early on the morning of February 23, 1945. Credited weeks later with being a first-flag-raiser—on the sole basis of one photograph reportedly showing his right arm and hand gripping the first flagpole—Charlo was shot to death during a company advance on March 2 and thus never knew of the credit.[8] A case has been made that he returned to the volcano's summit in the wake of the Schrier patrol's ascent, but in 2016, a Marine Corps investigation[9] was able to confirm that Charlo was *not* a flag-raiser, and his name was removed from the official list of first-flag-raisers. Louis Charlo is buried in Lake County, Montana.[10]

After Lieutenant Keith Wells was painfully wounded on February 22, Platoon Sergeant Boots Thomas ran Company E's 3rd Platoon with a relentless aggression against the Japanese. March 3, 1945, a week short of Thomas's 21st birthday, found the 28th Marines on the V Amphibious Corps far left flank, locked in the combat of attrition for the approaches to a large piece of heavily defended high ground dubbed Nishi Ridge. Here, as elsewhere, the Marines had the tactical edge gleaned from a strategy of movement versus the static defense the less operationally agile Japanese had opted to follow to the bitter end. Thomas was on his feet, directing his troops in the assault, when Private Phil Ward handed him a field telephone. Immediately, a sniper shot the handset (or, some said, his rifle) out of the young platoon leader's right hand. Unflappable in the face of danger, Thomas did not react. A second bullet followed the first and struck him in the mouth. Twenty-year-old Boots Thomas collapsed into himself, dead before he knew it.[11]

During a lull in the March 3 ordeal of advancing around the left (seaward) flank of Nishi Ridge, Lieutenant Colonel Chandler Johnson was, as usual, forward with the 2nd Battalion, 28th Marines' forward-most elements. Habitually aggressive, the 39-year-old 1929 Naval Academy graduate was pumping his troops up for another advance. Tanks were moving forward to help, and at least one 37mm gun was being manhandled into position to fire into the entrances of several Japanese-held caves. Soon, the tanks were halted before a wide, deep antitank ditch. Slowly, painstakingly, engineers moved forward to bulldoze a path to the floor of the antitank ditch while demolitions assault men and flamethrower teams scaled Nishi Ridge to get at cave entrances and firing embrasures. It was during another lull in the fighting at the foot of the ridge—at almost exactly 1400 hours—that Chandler Johnson ran forward from his command post to see for himself what was going on and what could be done, perhaps to set an example and provide advice. No one knew quite what happened, but many witnesses believe that the friendly 37mm gun scored a direct hit on Johnson, who was quite literally blown to pieces. (It could as easily have been a Japanese weapon fired from a hidden embrasure on the immensely well-fortified high ground.) The brave and bravely led 2nd Battalion, 28th Marines, was stunned but not stalled. The attack continued, just as Chandler Johnson would have wished.[12]

> Lieutenant Colonel Chandler W. Johnson, USMC
> Navy Cross Citation:
> The President of the United States takes pride in presenting the Navy Cross (Posthumously) to Chandler W. Johnson (0-4434), Lieutenant Colonel, U.S. Marine Corps, for extraordinary heroism as Commanding Officer of the Second Battalion, Twenty-Eighth Marines, FIFTH Marine Division, during operations against enemy Japanese forces on Iwo Jima in the Volcano Islands, from 19 February to 2 March 1945. Landing his force in the wake of an assault battalion on D-Day, Lieutenant Colonel Johnson advanced his men against savage hostile resistance as they executed a difficult turning maneuver to protect the left flank of assault troops moving across the island and, completing this initial mission in a minimum of time, forged steadily onward to penetrate the intricate network of fortifications circling the base of Mount Suribachi. Scaling the steep, gun-studded face of the mountain, he maintained close control of operations, blasting the defending garrisons from their deeply-entrenched positions and seizing the volcanic stronghold with its commanding gun batteries on D-plus-4. With Mount Suribachi secured, Lieutenant Colonel Johnson waged a relentless drive northward toward the sea, smashing through seemingly impregnable Japanese defenses, fighting the enemy with indomitable force and annihilating them with inexorable determination. Gaining the rugged, difficult terrain north of Hill 362 on D-plus-11, he discovered that strongly fortified, well-concealed Japanese forces were inflicting heavy casualties on his forward companies. Instantly proceeding to the front lines, he fearlessly made his way among the besieged units, ordering corrective measures, rallying and reorganizing his stout-hearted fighters for renewed assault. Although instantly killed by a bursting mortar shell as he moved from the right assault company to the adjacent company's observation post, Lieutenant Colonel Johnson, by his outstanding valor, dynamic energies and skilled combat tactics in the face of tremendous odds, had inspired his men to heroic effort throughout twelve days of fierce conflict, thereby contributing essentially to the ultimate capture of this vital Japanese outpost. His brilliant leadership and astute military acumen throughout reflect the highest credit upon himself and the United States Naval Service. He gallantly gave his life for his country.

On March 4, a rainy, cloudy, misty day, Staff Sergeant Bill Genaust hauled his movie camera to the front line to either photograph or help Marines mop up on an especially stubbornly held hill. According to one source, Genaust and an infantryman entered a cave to escape the rain[13] while another source[14] indicates that the pair volunteered to reconnoiter the cave using Genaust's flashlight. As soon as the cameraman turned on the light, a Japanese machine gun hidden in the cave's interior cut him nearly in half and apparently killed the other Marine for good measure. Marines then outposted the entrance and the cave was sealed as soon as a bulldozer could be guided in. There was no point risking American lives to retrieve the bodies. When, the next day, friends of Genaust attempted to locate the cave's sealed entrance in order to retrieve the bodies, the area had become too jumbled by cave-sealing for Genaust's cave to be located, much less unsealed. Bill Genaust is thus carried on Marine Corps casualty rolls as missing in action. He never had an opportunity to see the film he shot on February 23. In 1995, his memory was honored by a plaque placed on the summit of Mount Suribachi.[15]

On March 9, elements of the 3rd Marine Division, in the V Amphibious Corps center, broke through to the coast around Kitano Point, in the far, far north of Iwo Jima. The breakthrough split the Japanese resistance and allowed the 3rd and 4th Marine divisions to turn from direct assault to mopping-up. The 5th Marine Division, on the V Amphibious Corps left (western) flank, still faced a battle of attrition to overcome a powerful and powerfully fortified zone of resistance.[16]

Pharmacist's Mate John Bradley's last battle was fought on March 12, as the 28th Marines continued to wade into nearly the last organized Japanese defensive zone on the island.[17] Bradley was huddled at the base of a cliff with a handful of Marines who were all convinced the cover behind an overhang was good.

"It was just about evening," Bradley reported five weeks later.[18] "I was getting things squared around my foxhole, getting my medical gear and personal gear arranged so that at night, if we got the word to move out, I'd know just where everything was ... [T]hings were entirely quiet up to this time. While I was arranging this, a Jap mortar shell [hit] several feet from me ... [I]t caught four men, and I happened to be one of them."

The mortar round smashed into the rock and spread shrapnel out and downward, beneath the overhang. One man, who was blinded by the shrapnel, had to be pulled back under cover by Bradley, who had himself been struck by multiple shrapnel shards in his right foot, calf, and thigh. Although he had been badly injured and was losing blood from many wounds, he turned to assist a Marine whose legs had been even more badly injured. Then he helped the blinded man to a nearby aid station. In all, a badly bleeding Doc Bradley ran hither and yon to treat at least five Marines who had suffered shrapnel wounds from the one mortar round.[19]

Captain Dave Severance later wrote that he personally saw Bradley racing around to treat the wounded while studiously ignoring his own bleeding wounds. "It would be hard to estimate the number of lives he saved by his skillful administration of medical aid, carried out with complete disregard for his own safety ..."[20]

In the end, Bradley was rushed to a front-line aid station, then on to a field hospital. The worst of the steel shards were removed from the array of wounds before he was loaded the next morning onto a medical evacuation flight to Guam for a higher level of treatment. He was flown to the Honolulu naval hospital via the stopover on Guam, then to the Oakland, California, naval hospital, where he had served earlier in the war. By then, millions of copies of the Rosenthal photo were flooding America's newspapers and magazines, but a wounded Doc Bradley traveled in complete anonymity. No one appeared to know who the men raising the flag were in real life. Or real death.[21]

On March 13, Private First Class René Gagnon fired his rifle for the first time on Iwo Jima. He and a fellow Marine wandered into a cave behind the front lines that they assumed hid no Japanese. This was a classic error that claimed an unknowable number of American lives on Iwo Jima. The solitary Japanese soldier aimed his rifle at the Marines and prepared to fire. While Gagnon hesitated to consider why he was in a position to kill a fellow human being, the Japanese soldier shot the other Marine dead in his tracks. Before the enemy soldier could adjust his aim, Gagnon fired a single, fatal, round.[22]

On March 14, Lieutenant General Holland Smith ordered a new American flag to be formally—and officially—raised over Kitano Point, in farthest northern Iwo Jima. The by-then weather-beaten second Suribachi flag—the *Rosenthal* flag—was lowered as soon as the new flag was up.[23] Ironically, the substitute Suribachi flag became *the* flag as its smaller twin receded from the public consciousness.[24]

Also on March 14, the battle-weary 4th Marine Division began a slow withdrawal from the shrinking front lines to prepare to leave the island.[25]

The U.S. Army's Iwo Jima occupation force, an independent regimental combat team, arrived offshore on March 20 to begin replacing Marine units then mopping up the 3rd and 4th Marine division zones.[26]

Private First Class Franklin Sousley was shot on March 21, 1945. He had the so-called "thousand-yard stare" leading up to the incident, a symptom indicating that his fine-tuned self-preservation instincts had been temporarily—or permanently—overwhelmed by the unremitting grind of full immersion into violence and death. Nearly the Kentuckian's last act was cradling the head of a mortally wounded man. Possibly, that was Sousley's breaking point. The next thing his comrades knew, he was wandering onto an open path known for its excellent sniper vistas, probably not focusing on much of anything. It was late afternoon; Company E's 2nd Platoon had been fully engaged since sun-up.

The sniper's bullet struck Sousley while all the Marines nearby dove for cover. He swatted at his back as if he had been stung by a bee. Then he toppled onto the roadway.

A Marine nearby called out, "How you doin'?"

Sousley answered with his final words, his final breath: "Not bad. I don't feel anything."

Franklin Sousley was the final Iwo Jima flag-raiser to die in the war. He never knew of the notoriety he would be accorded.[27]

Sousley was buried in the 5th Marine Division Cemetery on Iwo Jima, then reinterred in the Elizaville, Kentucky, cemetery.[28]

During the wee hours of March 26, 1945, Japanese troops mounted a desperate assault on Marines pinning them into the uncleared northwestern pocket of resistance as well as Marine and Army Air Forces airmen sleeping in tents at the nearest airfield. The whole venture, which was hair-raising for those who were involved or threatened, came to nothing.

The battle for Iwo Jima was formally ended at 0930 hours on March 26 and responsibility for securing the island was formally turned over by V Amphibious Corps to the U.S. Army occupation troops.

Fifth Marine Division survivors held a memorial service at the division cemetery on their way to embark for Hawaii, and they were all off the island the next day, March 27, looking ahead to rebuilding the division for the upcoming invasion of the main Japanese home islands.[29]

CHAPTER 8

After

Bluff

Warrant Officer Norman Hatch, the 5th Marine Division photo officer, was ordered to fly to Los Angeles from Iwo Jima on March 9, 1945. His immediate task was to deliver all of the raw film exposed by the Marine Corps cinematographers from three Marine divisions between February 27 and his date of departure, then to move on to Washington, D.C., to await further instructions. All of the Iwo Jima film footage was for use in a documentary movie already signed for production by Warner Brothers and distribution by United Artists. During his time in Washington, Hatch expected to be grilled by all-comers for everything he knew or might know about the roiling so-called Joe Rosenthal "staged" flag-raising photo.[1] Among the reels of exposed movie film Hatch had dropped off in Los Angeles was Sergeant Bill Genaust's footage on the second flag-raising, which no one on Earth saw until Hollywood technicians developed it.

Norm Hatch was the right man for the jobs he had been given; for four days in late November 1943, Technical Sergeant Hatch had braved sheets of Japanese gunfire to train his trusty 16mm Eyemo movie camera on horrific combat action. He was thus able to shoot a few seconds of extremely rare footage—perhaps the *first* footage—showing Japanese and U.S. Marine combat infantrymen in the same frames. After Tarawa, he had had a hand in working on a bluntly accurate documentary movie using, in the main, film he had shot. He had also been invited to confer directly with President Franklin Roosevelt over whether the American public could accept the unvarnished gory details of the first documentary movie to focus on an amphibious assault in the Pacific. His comment—to the effect that "Tarawa was the first of many such bloody assaults. We have to face up to the cost sooner or later."—helped sway the

President to allow the censors to pass the movie for release. *With the Marines at Tarawa* won the 1944 Academy Award for best short documentary, and 23-year-old Norm Hatch was there, in Hollywood, to help accept the Oscar in behalf of his fellow United States Marines. Thanks in part to Norm Hatch, the American public did indeed embrace and overcome the inevitable sad lesson the film carried in every frame.[2]

Now, in March 1945, with the invasion of Japan looming in everyone's minds, Hatch had been detailed to help put together a documentary that would focus on how the war had evolved into new heights of bitter, bloody exchanges between grudge-carrying young men who would be fighting on blood-drenched Japanese soil.

As soon as Warrant Officer Hatch arrived in the nation's capital—it took him seven days from Iwo despite his having the highest possible travel authority[3]—he was shanghaied to a meeting with General Alexander Vandegrift, the commandant of the Marine Corps. Also waiting to meet Hatch in the commandant's office was Alan J. Gould—the Associated Press executive editor—and several Time-Life and AP senior personnel. They all wanted to know, once and for all, about the legitimacy of the Rosenthal photo.

Hatch gave his assurances that, based on his talks with Bill Genaust and Bob Campbell, Rosenthal took his shot at the moment both flags were set in motion, one up and one down.[4] This affirmation led to official recognition of The Photo by the Marine Corps and the national press.

General Vandegrift viewed the relieved release of breath in the room as an opportunity to broach a matter of crass commercialism. He asked the AP executive editor, Alan Gould, for permission to use the Rosenthal image in the perennial Marine Corps recruiting effort.

"You can have two duplicate negatives," Gould rejoined, "and every print will cost you one dollar."

It was a standard Hollywood deal, but the room nevertheless went dead silent. A discomforting tightening of muscles might have momentarily engulfed the commandant's brow.

Vandegrift broke the brief silence by asking Hatch for an opinion of Gould's offer.

Hatch spoke the truth when he revealed that he had delivered Bill Genaust's movie film of the second flag-raising to the Warner Brothers' studio in Hollywood,[5] but not so much when he implied he had seen the film. He had not; it had yet to be developed. But he went on to mention that "we could blow [the best frame of the movie film] up to eight-by-ten [inches] and make a print to it. And, yes, we'll lose some definition that way, but the footage belongs to us and so we wouldn't need to pay."

Gould fell for it. Not only hadn't Hatch seen the Genaust footage, none of the film Hatch had dragged back home from Iwo had yet been processed. For all anyone on Earth knew, the flag-raising footage might all have been ruined by damage, scratching, underexposure, etc. There might be nothing of value.

But Gould didn't notice that he was being bluffed. All he could fathom was that he had been trumped by the roll of movie film Bill Genaust had exposed atop Suribachi. He might be looking foolish or, worse, he and his employer might be denounced for war profiteering or impeding morale. And so Jay Gould caved in, utterly. He agreed to turn over to the Marine Corps a direct copy of Joe Rosenthal's original flag-raising negative as well as free use of the image "in perpetuity" as long as AP was credited. It was a major concession that would and did bolster morale, and it saved the Marine Corps millions, or maybe billions, of dollars in licensing fees down through the decades—or at least did not incentivize the Marine Corps to cancel its planned use of the expensive image.

Hatch's opinion of The Photo: "It's a picture that tells a story. It shows the urgency of getting that flag up. It's got a feeling in it."[6]

The Iwo Jima documentary, *To the Shores of Iwo Jima*, was released on June 7, 1945. It was nominated for an Academy Award but did not win.

Hatch was in Hawaii, newly appointed as the 2nd Marine Division photo officer and tasked with preparing for Operation Olympic, the invasion of Kyushu, the southernmost main Japanese home island. He was watching a movie in Honolulu when the projector stopped and people's voices caught his attention. The hubbub announced the detonation of something called an atomic bomb over the Japanese city of Hiroshima. A few days later, Norm Hatch was on his way to document the effects on humans and cities in the wake of both atomic explosions. Radiation was a consideration, but lead was not: Emperor Hirohito had agreed to an unconditional surrender and his military chiefs did not stand in the way. Warrant Officer Norm Hatch was one of millions of American servicemen who felt they had been given a new lease on life.[7]

The Memorial

It must have been a giant cosmic joke that Felix de Weldon ended his U.S. Navy war-time service as a Painter Second Class. But that was because the navy offered its sailors no option to specialize in fine arts and sculpture. Thus, painter second class it was as the fine artist worked just as hard to win the war as the sailors who painted ships and buildings, airplanes and signs.

Long before he enlisted in the U.S. Navy, Dr. Felix de Weldon was a world-renowned Austrian painter and sculptor who had been classically trained at the University of Vienna's Academy of Creative Arts and School of Architecture. As a child, he was regarded as a prodigy; in 1929, at the age of 17, he completed his first commission for a notable's bust, and at 18 he sculpted the monument for U.S. President Herbert Hoover's children's relief program in Europe. Young de Weldon earned a master's degree in art and science and a doctorate in architecture by the age of twenty-two. He next studied archaeology at Oxford University.[8]

De Weldon left Austria permanently in 1933, settled in England, and found himself in Canada in 1937 to sculpt a bust of that nation's prime minister. During a whirlwind tour of 44 U.S. states, de Weldon fell in love with the United States and settled there.[9]

Though otherwise qualified to be a commissioned officer, de Weldon was technically an enemy alien throughout his war-time naval tour and therefore could not become an officer right off. (He was finally cleared and offered a commission as lieutenant commander shortly after the war ended, but if he accepted, he would have had to postpone his departure for two years. Lucrative art commissions awaited, so he mustered out at his enlisted rank.)[10]

Painter Second Class de Weldon was transferred in 1943 to the newly established naval air station at Patuxent River, Maryland, and placed under the direct supervision of the base executive officer, Commander Thurston "T. B." Clark. The job was to search for combat photos that could serve as subject matter for heroic naval aviation paintings to be executed by de Weldon. He was the official artist for naval aviation, but Commander Clark, a United States Naval Academy graduate and blooded combat veteran, joined him to search for suitable naval aviation subject matter almost daily from among the haul of new photographic submissions. According to de Weldon,

[On February 23, 1945,] which was twenty-four hours behind the 23rd of February on Iwo Jima, [a] wire photo … was sent from Hawaii to our naval air station, because we had an annex to the photo lab in Anacostia and whenever these battle pictures came in, our executive officer, Commander T. B. Clark, … called me to his office to look over these battle pictures to see if any were worthy of being permanently painted for the Naval Academy or for the Navy Archives. At that time I was painting the battle of the Coral Sea.

When I saw the picture of the Iwo Jima flag raising, I was so deeply impressed by its significance, its meaning, that I imagined that it would arouse the imagination of the American people to show the forward drive, the unison of action, the will to sacrifice, the relentless determination of these young men. Everything was embodied in that picture. At that time I asked Commander Clark if I could discontinue for a few days the work on the battle of the Coral Sea and make a [maquette, a scale model] of the flag raising. And he said to go right ahead. That was a Friday. I worked all Friday night, all Saturday, part of Saturday night, all Sunday, and, by Monday morning, the [wax] model was completed.[11]

As much as he saw the strength of The Photo as a means to raise patriotic ardor, de Weldon was also deeply impressed by the photo as art, by its adherence to what his long years of training in Europe had taught him about ancient and classic heroic art. The Photo appeared to offer the perfect classic lines—the pyramidal base, the flagpole caught at a 45-degree angle—to serve, right out of the box, as a template for a massive, heroic sculpture.[12]

After de Weldon's superiors viewed the small wax sculpture, the artist was dispatched to nearby Washington to meet with the chief of naval operations, Admiral Louis Denfeld. From there, the sculptor was escorted by four U.S. Navy captains to be interviewed by the commandant of the Marine Corps, General Alexander Vandegrift.

Vandegrift said, when the wax sculpture was brought into his office on a table cart, "Of course, this model will stay right here." At which one of the captains piped up, "We have given our word to [Admiral Denfeld] to bring it back."

Brigadier General Robert Denig, the Marine Corps' chief public information officer, told General Vandegrift that he had had a phone call from an official representing secretary of the treasury Henry Morganthau, Jr., to the effect that the treasury department wanted to use the Iwo Jima flag-raising image as the symbol for the next Victory Bond drive, and to learn if a larger model could be made for the launching of that.

"So they asked me," de Weldon recalled, "if I could make a larger model. And being an enlisted man, all I could say was, 'Aye, aye, sir.' That's when I started to work on the next model. [For that,] I had the three survivors posing for me for their own likenesses. In that model the figures were one and a half times life-sized, nine feet tall, and it was dedicated on November 10, 1945, in front of the Navy Department [building] … and that launched the Victory Bond drive. It was a combined project of the Marines and the U.S. Treasury. It stood there until 1948…. [I]n the meantime, a joint resolution was passed by Congress to make that symbolic flag raising the national monument for the United States Marine Corps, but the Marines didn't want any public funds, they only wanted permission to put the monument on public land, and they said they could raise the funds…. [T]he Marine Corps [War] Memorial Foundation was formed … and the money was raised. Altogether, there were thirty-six different studies for the big monument. All these thirty-six different studies have been placed either in museums or military bases or public places."[13]

Dr. de Weldon was mustered out of the navy upon completion of his four-year enlistment. He went straight to work as a freelance painter and sculptor. He was drawn back to work on the flag-raising sculpture in 1951, when the Marine Corps War Memorial Foundation was ready for his participation. Over the next three years, hundreds of assistants were hired to plan and execute the commission.[14] The groundbreaking ceremony was held on February 19, 1954, the ninth anniversary (plus one day) of the raising of the flag on Iwo Jima.[15]

The colossal bronze monument was dedicated on November 10, 1954, the 179th anniversary of the founding of the United States Marine Corps. The human figures are 32 feet tall—four stories.[16]

In addition to Washington bigwigs and major donors, those in prominent attendance included John Bradley, René Gagnon, and Ira Hayes. Much farther down the ceremonial food chain—given seating but otherwise ignored—were several first-flag notables, including Lou Lowery, George Schrier, James Michels, and Chuck Lindberg.[17]

In June 12, 1961, President John F. Kennedy took the rare step of ordering that the U.S. national colors be flown over the Marine Corps Memorial twenty-four hours a day. Not known to perhaps a majority of visitors to the site and to Marines in general, the so-called "Iwo Jima Memorial" is dedicated "In Honor And Memory Of The Men Of The United States Marine Corps Who Have Given Their Lives To Their Country Since 10 November 1775."[18]

CHAPTER 9

The Mighty 7th

Confusion and Exploitation

It appears that Congressman Mike Mansfield of Montana—the home state of purported first-flag-raiser Louis Charlo—was the first to propose that the flag-raisers be invited to join the 7th War Bond troupe, which was not yet fully filled out. That was on March 7, the day former Marine Mansfield took to the floor of the House of Representatives to propose the inclusion of the flag-raisers and suggest that the image in the widely disseminated and instantly iconic Rosenthal flag-raising photo be used as a symbol of the bond drive.

Like many ebullient Americans at the time—before anyone in authority even thought to identify any of the flag-raisers—Mansfield was led astray by news articles ascribing the flag-raising to the four-man Watson patrol, which undertook the first American effort to reconnoiter the trail to Suribachi's summit. Thus, it is evident that Mansfield, among many others, was not only not yet aware that two flags had been raised, but that he was led to believe the erroneous early news reports that linked the Watson patrol to the flag-raising. The fact that Louis Charlo was a life-long resident of Mansfield's district (as was the entire population of sparsely settled Montana) no doubt provided a great deal of the impetus for Mansfield's avidity to throw more light on the young man. As well, the fact that Charlo was killed in action on March 3 just made the bid to lionize him appear all the more fitting.[1]

And Representative Mansfield was not alone in milking the good will of the American people to call attention to the flag-raising. A week before Mansfield's proposal was made on the House floor, the Florida congressman representing Boots Thomas's district had proposed that a national war memorial based on the Rosenthal photo be funded by the Congress. (There is no evidence to suggest that this congressman knew that Felix de Weldon was already working on just such a statue.) Two weeks later, a senator proposed that the post office be directed to issue a postage stamp using the Rosenthal image. And on and on. Officialdom piled on with attention-getting schemes to exploit the flag-raising and the flag-raisers, some with altruistic intentions, most with cynical intentions, many with both.

Further, as the flag-raising news slowly oozed out, news editors were becoming increasingly curious about who the flag-raisers were, specifically. If that eagerness had only been fueled by an impulse to sell more papers and advertising, the push for facts would have been amply justified, but the apparent impulse to raise the spirits of tens of millions of war-weary Americans was a better way to justify the ongoing, increasingly urgent probes for specific names.

On March 23, just as public interest first showed signs of stalling, Technical Sergeant Keyes Beech, the irrepressible public information operative who, the day after the flags went up, launched a brief campaign to lionize Boots Thomas as *the* hero of the flag-raising, came forward with a list of five possible *second*-flag-raisers: Doc Bradley, René Gagnon, Hank Hansen, Franklin Sousley, and Mike Strank. And, though Thomas was not named on this list, Beech's efforts to raise Thomas's image in the immediate aftermath of the flag-raising had by late March taken on a life of their own, especially with the assists from politicians who had something to sell.[2]

The Presidential Call

Once the connection between the flag-raising and the upcoming war-bond drive was pointed out to him—apparently as the public's interest in Iwo Jima appeared to wane—President Franklin Roosevelt perceived so much public relations value in The Photo that he readily accepted the suggestion that the flag-raisers shown in it be added to the cast of the new 7th War Bond drive, then gathering steam in its planning stage. (It is not clear if Roosevelt was yet aware that two flags had been raised over Suribachi, or that almost everyone appeared to be focusing on the beautifully photographed second one.) Certain that fresh-faced young servicemen newly returned from the front lines would be able to help engineer an immense financial success story, on March 30 the President ordered the surviving flag-raisers—first flag, second flag, who knew?—to be identified and transported to Washington, D.C., post-haste, to take part in a plan to raise $13 billion in voluntary contributions from a population not yet fully over the Great Depression, much less over immersion in a global war.

By the time President Roosevelt personally interceded, three of the six second-flag-raisers had been killed in action, Iwo Jima had been declared secure, and the 5th Marine Division was on its way back to Hawaii by ship.

Identifying the Flag-raisers

You have to wonder how collecting five or six names of Marines from one's own infantry company could go so completely off the rails. But there was a war on, and, in the hell that is war, any little thing could interfere with the ability to get stuff right. One example of a "little thing" came out when Lieutenant George Schrier, among others, was *ordered* to submit a complete list of the second-flag-raisers so news reporters could identify them for their readers and listeners. By then Schrier, who had paid no attention to the raising of the second flag and thus had no direct knowledge at the time of who those men were, was deeply and emotionally immersed in commanding the 2nd Battalion, 28th Marines' Company D in the drive to the north end of Iwo Jima. At times testy while under pressure, Schrier is said to have scribbled four names—not the required five or six—on a sheet of paper as a protest before he closed himself off from an investigation he had never really supported or felt was necessary.[3] He later commented, "At the time the picture was taken, I was busy taking down the original flag and cannot definitively identify any member [of] the second flag-raising."[4]

The battle for Iwo Jima itself accounted for more loss of momentum in getting any information from the two living and self-acknowledged second-flag-raisers—René Gagnon and John Bradley (but not Ira Hayes, who denied his role). When asked to pull possible participants and witnesses off the line to be interviewed during the closing days of fighting, Captain Dave Severance stood squarely in the way. Company E, which was slowly and expensively taking ground along the island's western coast, on the V Amphibious Corps and 5th Marine Division far left flank, was down to two thin platoons, around 20 men each on an average day—mostly scared replacements, many of whom were too mortified by the death all around them to lift their heads even to observe the battlefield on which they were barely surviving. There were not enough veterans left in the company to set an example of confidence or ease the tyros into forming the habits that kept most infantrymen reasonably safe most of the time. Moreover, Severance reckoned that giving his putative flag-raisers a few hours or a day off might be tantamount to sending them to their deaths. The company commander well knew that it was often as dangerous to be in the rear—or moving between the rear and the front—as it was to be on the front. So any member of Company E who might be a second-flag-raiser became off limits as long as the company was in action—as long as Company E's commanding officer had bigger things to worry about.[5]

Although it eventually came to light that four members of a single rifle squad had had their hands on the improvised flagpole when it went up, it was nevertheless a pick-up work detail that raised the second flag. As far as anyone who was still alive could remember, perhaps one of the sergeants at the scene—Hansen or Strank—acting on orders from George Schrier, counted off a few nearby Marines and told them to lend a hand. Why would anyone ask or note who helped out at the flagpole, especially the second-string flagpole? The exigencies of war kept everyone fit and busy. (By the same token, 70-plus years would pass before the identities of those who actually raised the first flag would be officially determined.) Why would any temporary grouping like the two ordered to raise heavy makeshift flagpoles even take note of themselves? It wasn't as if there was fame involved. Or bonus pay, or overtime, or a steak dinner, or even an attaboy attached to the job. These were mud Marines; they didn't rate even a brusque thank-you. Working stiffs obedient to orders in ever-changing groupings, they greased the skids of war, formed and unformed work details and ad hoc assault groups a thousand times a day without fanfare, recognition, or much comment—or even remembering they had.

The second flag-raising was so devoid of importance at the time that no one—ever—has been able to place an accurate time on it. Some figured it might have happened between 1400 and 1430; others thought it took place at around 1230. But these were guesses made long after detailed memory faded, because the event of the second flag-raising fell beneath notice in the 2nd Battalion's February 23 after-action report entry.[6]

We, who have witnessed this 70-plus-year effort to collect the *correct* names of merely six flag-raisers, all assumed a lot over the ups and downs of those decades. No one took notes; they just fell in as ordered to perform a routine task requiring grunt labor. This one, the one with the flag, was a halfway useful routine task followed by an impromptu celebration (the Gung Ho photo), followed by more work or more fighting as soon as the Gung Ho crowd scattered to the wind. It wasn't until after The Photo gained notoriety and presidential notice graced it that anyone in authority attempted to systematically piece it all together, and that took place because of pressure from newsmen who were looking to promote human-interest stories for their readers. It was only then—weeks after the fact—that *that* job, the *flag* job, was pretty much a long-shot memory exercise from odds and sods who were there *and still alive*—for nearly half of all the men who raised both flags, real

Two Flags Over Iwo Jima, February 23, 1945

A Hike to the Summit

Lieutenant Colonel Chandler Johnson (facing camera with phone in hand) greets the Company E patrol at his bare-bones forward command post. Facing Johnson, with helmet on, is 1st Lieutenant George Schrier, and, behind Schrier, wearing a soft cover and holding a cigarette, is 1st Lieutenant George Greeley Wells. Suribachi looms in the background. Johnson is requesting via phone that naval gunfire against targets on Suribachi be shut down for the duration of the patrol. (Official USMC photo by Staff Sergeant Lou Lowery)

Company E's reinforced 3rd Platoon approaches Suribachi's base. Note the impressions of tank tracks, no doubt from an abortive attempt to gain a toehold, but there is zero opposition facing the 45-man Schrier patrol this day. (Official USMC photo by Staff Sergeant Lou Lowery)

The Schrier patrol faces steep terrain as it passes the corpse of a Japanese soldier. (Official USMC photo by Staff Sergeant Lou Lowery)

A bit rattled by the lack of opposition, Sergeant Lowery requests an opportunity to mark the moment with a photo of the flag, just in case. (Official USMC photo by Staff Sergeant Lou Lowery)

The Schrier patrol vanguard takes cover at a well-maintained but abandoned dual-purpose antiaircraft gun position near Suribachi's summit. The Marine at far left is Sergeant Hank Hansen, the man to his immediate right is Lieutenant Schrier, and the radioman Private First Class Ray Jacobs. (Official USMC photo by Staff Sergeant Lou Lowery)

The patrol sets into defensive positions. The prone Marine nearest the camera is Private First Class Harold Schultz. (Official USMC photo by Staff Sergeant Lou Lowery)

Raising the First Flag

Seen here, left to right: Lieutenant George Schrier, Platoon Sergeant Boots Thomas, Sergeant Hank Hansen, and Corporal Chuck Lindberg. (Official USMC photo by Staff Sergeant Lou Lowery)

Five of the six first-flag raisers wait while Corporal Chuck Lindberg begins carving a hole for the flagpole by digging divots with the heel of his right boondocker. Left to right: First Lieutenant George Schrier's helmet, Corporal Lindberg, Pharmacist's Mate John Bradley (note the medical bags at his hips), Private Phil Ward, Sergeant Hank Hansen, and Platoon Sergeant Boots Thomas. (Official USMC photo by Staff Sergeant Lou Lowery

The first-flag raisers pause for a group portrait. Left to right are Corporal Lindberg; Sergeant Howard Snyder (who provided security); Doc Bradley; Private Ward; Platoon Sergeant Thomas; Sergeant Hansen; Private First Class Ray Jacobs (radioman); and, seated to use the radio, Lieutenant Schrier. (Official USMC photo by Staff Sergeant Lou Lowery)

This is the most familiar photo of the first-flag raising. The Marine standing watch in the foreground is Private First Class James Michels. In the background, at far left, is Ray Jacobs; seated on the ground behind Jacobs' legs, is George Schrier; wearing his soft cover is Hank Hansen (whose left hand is second from the top on the flagpole; with only his helmet and right hand showing (third from top) is Phil Ward, who was misidentified as Louis Charlo until 2008; with both hands (top and bottom hands on the flagpole) and most of his head showing is Doc Bradley; kneeling in front of Bradley is Boots Thomas; and standing at far right, behind Michels, is Chuck Lindberg. (Official USMC photo by Staff Sergeant Lou Lowery)

Raising the Second Flag

The first flag (foreground) comes down as the larger second flag goes up. (Official USMC photo by Private Robert Campbell)

What Joe Rosenthal's camera saw: The Photo as taken, before it was cropped by an Associated Press photo editor on Guam. (Joe Rosenthal)

Raising the Flag On Iwo Jima. (Joe Rosenthal)

Hand salute: At left is George Schrier, at right is Boots Thomas. (Official USMC photo)

In Joe Rosenthal's second of three photos taken atop Suribachi, Private First Class Ira Hayes (left), Private First Class Franklin Sousley (center), Sergeant Mike Strank (mostly hidden), and Corporal Harlon Block (far right) hold the flagpole steady while other Marines search for lines to anchor the flag against the wind atop Suribachi. This photo was helpful in 2016 in making a corrected identification of Sousley in the Rosenthal flag-raising photo. (Associated Press photo by Joe Rosenthal)

Joe Rosenthal takes his third—the infamous "Gung Ho"—photo atop Suribachi. Note the stones he is using to gain height. Beside Rosenthal's left leg is Sergeant Bill Genaust, with his movie camera in action. (Official USMC photo by Private Robert Campbell)

The Gung Ho photo. (Associated Press photo by Joe Rosenthal)

Joe Rosenthal and Bob Campbell stop for a break on their way down the volcano. (Official USMC photo)

Father Charles Suver officiates at an impromptu mass atop Suribachi. (Official USMC photo)

The hard-won vista from atop Suribachi. (Official USMC photo)

Mopping Up, February 24 and 25, 1945

Clearing the way for engineers and flamethrower teams, Marine infantrymen suppress fire from a concrete pillbox laid bare by Marine artillery or naval gunfire, or both. (Official USMC photo)

Two Combat Team 28 flamethrower operators burn out a Japanese defensive structure at Suribachi's base. (Official USMC photo)

Another bunker at Suribachi's base is atomized by bunker-busting teams of flamethrower operators, engineers, and infantrymen. (Official USMC photo)

Fame

Lieutenant General Holland M. Smith welcomes Platoon Sergeant Ernest "Boots" Thomas aboard the USS *Eldorado* on February 24, 1945. Thomas did not know that he was auditioning for the part of America's national hero. (Official USMC photo)

President Harry Truman greets visitors to the Oval Office: (left to right) Dr. Felix de Weldon, sculptor of the model for what became the Marine Corps War Memorial; Joe Rosenthal; and Lieutenant Colonel Edward Haganeh, deputy director of Marine Corps Public Information. (Official White House photo)

Now All Together.

Still recuperating from leg wounds sustained on Iwo Jima, U.S. Navy Pharmacist's Mate 2nd Class John Bradley eases into his new role as fundraiser. (Official Marine Corps photo)

While on tour as part of the 7th War Bond Drive, the three surviving second-flag raisers—left to right: Ira Hayes, John Bradley, and Rene Gagnon—pose with the actual second flag raised over Suribachi. (Official USMC photo)

On November 10, 1954, Bradley, Hayes, and Gagnon were the guests of honor for the dedication of the long-awaited Marine Corps War Memorial in Arlington, Virginia. It was the last time all three saw one another. (Official USMC photo)

The Marine Corps War Memorial, where the U.S. National Colors fly all day every day. (Official USMC photo)

or otherwise, were in their graves by the time orders came from on high to identify and locate the second-flag-raisers, then get them safely home to the United States to take part in the latest war-bond drive.

Trouble and Bother

The trouble began almost immediately. Private First Class René Gagnon, the Company E runner entrusted by Lieutenant Colonel Chandler Johnson with getting the large second flag to Suribachi's summit—and delivering the first flag back to Johnson's command post—was known by battalion and regimental officers at the outset of the search to have had a hand in raising the second flag. This was initially a supposition based on the fact that Gagnon had been entrusted with carrying the second flag to the volcano's summit. After acknowledging that he had indeed helped raise the second flag, the Company E runner was almost immediately drawn into the search for the four or five unidentified participants in raising the second flag (which had taken on more importance than the *very important* first flag owing to (a) the swift public release of the Rosenthal flag-raising photo, (b) the powerful, if lucky artistry of the Rosenthal's photo of the second flag-raising, and (c) the importance President Roosevelt was placing on the Rosenthal photo itself as a financial boon—the money shot—to the upcoming 7th War Bond Drive).

During the first leg of the ocean journey from Iwo Jima to Hawaii,[7] Gagnon—who was working the flag puzzle under the general direction of Captain Fred Haynes, who had risen to become the 28th Marines operations officer—was accosted by Private First Class Ira Hayes.

Having witnessed the national fervor for the Rosenthal flag-raising photo, even from such isolated vantage points as Iwo Jima and a troopship at sea, Hayes clearly anticipated that fame would be unleashed on the second-flag-raisers. Unaware that he had already been halfway implicated, along with Sousley, in the second flag-raising, Hayes told Gagnon that he simply wanted no part in the hoopla and would harm Gagnon if Gagnon named him. Sufficiently motivated, Gagnon made a point of *not* naming Hayes.[8]

With Hayes's threat firmly implanted in his mind, Gagnon had gone about the business of identifying the other second-flag-raisers even though he had personally arrived at Suribachi's summit with the four members of Company E's 2nd Platoon who had run telephone wire to George Schrier on February 23. The 2nd Platoon men and Gagnon had arrived on the summit in the midst of a widening pilgrimage and burgeoning flurry of activity, so their presence might not have registered with Schrier or any of the 3rd Platoon men, but surely they registered with Gagnon, who was shoulder-to-shoulder with them when the second flag was raised. Yet the men Gagnon had identified so far to Captain Haynes as second-flag-raisers were himself, Sergeant Michael Strank, and Private First Class Franklin Sousley. Ira Hayes had warned Gagnon to leave him out of it.

Another name that had come to Gagnon, from an unknown source (but possibly Technical Sergeant Beech) was Sergeant Hank Hansen, the 3rd Platoon right guide. Hansen was a confirmed first-flag-raiser who had been killed the same day as Mike Strank, March 1. (It is also possible that Gagnon implicated Hansen simply to get out from under the pressure to name names.)

Until that point, the photo was ambiguous regarding the number of flag-raisers. It looked like five, but it might have been six. It was the evening before Gagnon was to leave the ship during a brief stopover at Eniwetok, in the western Marshall Islands. He had orders to catch a priority flight to the West Coast and on to Washington, D.C., so he could participate in the preparations for the 7th War Bond Drive.[9] Ira Hayes joined him outside the 28th Marines operations compartment and went on record as a flag-raiser (even though Gagnon had signed an affidavit asserting the man was not). Captain Fred Haynes dug out a Rosenthal flag-raising photo to aid Hayes in demonstrating that the ambiguity—five or six men in the photo—was erased if hands were counted; there were enough hands showing for six men.[10] Ultimately, though Hayes remained cool toward the fame that he faced, he agreed to let his part in the second flag-raising stand. Sometime later, an officer gave Gagnon a new affidavit to sign, this one confirming Hayes's actual role.

Gagnon arrived in Washington on April 7, initially to be debriefed by senior Marine Corps officers as well as to be available for press briefings and to prepare to take part in a busy, grinding war-bond tour. While Gagnon was billeted near Headquarters, Marine Corps, in Arlington, Virginia, Doc Bradley was quietly transferred from the Oakland naval hospital to Washington's Bethesda National Naval Medical Center to continue treatment of his wounds[11]—he was able to ambulate on crutches—while he attended briefings in the area.

So that made six second-flag-raisers: Gagnon, Hayes, and Bradley in the alive column and Hansen, Strank, and Sousley in the deceased column.

Who They Were

All looked to be hardened warriors, all were photogenic. One secret to the enduring popularity of the Rosenthal photo is the youthful, healthy, wholesome working-class posture and power of the flag-raisers. They represented the young

American warriors as recognizable individuals who had fought the Japanese to a standstill in 1942, opened the trans-Pacific offensive in 1943, reached Japan itself in 1944 via bomber bases they had captured on far-off Pacific islands—Saipan, Tinian, and Guam. And they had just conquered a tiny, distant—some would say strategically important—part of Japan itself, albeit on one of the Empire's farthest and loneliest outposts. In what had become the final push to the shores of the Japanese home islands, the working-man mud Marines were in the ascendant, poised to win. This was *their* moment and The Photo was *their* portrait, a moment and a portrait of pride in which the war-weary American public could share and draw sustenance and hope for victory in the nearest term. This was the message of the second flag. The Photo thus demonstrates the growing American confidence from fighting and winning on a worldwide stage and provided a map for the future. In the 50 years following World War II, the American worker—the disciplined American *veteran*—came into his own as a sustaining influence in the burgeoning, kinetic American and global economies. This was also the message of the second flag.

The photo emphasizes teamwork, getting the job done together, a public spirit shared by men with similar experience of war. It is the very embodiment of "*work together*," what Marines mean when they say, "Gung ho," from the Mandarin *kung ho*.

An ill, physically exhausted President Roosevelt died suddenly on April 12, 1945, putting the flag-raisers' role in the 7th War Bond Drive in minor jeopardy of being overlooked by a desperately busy President Harry S. Truman. But Truman picked up the ball as soon as he was able; the war-bond money still needed to be collected and spent on the war.

On April 19, Gagnon and Bradley were on hand to greet Ira Hayes when he arrived in Washington, D.C., by plane from Hawaii. After settling in as a temporary member of 1st Headquarters Battalion, Headquarters, Marine Corps, Hayes was interviewed by a Marine lieutenant colonel who had already interviewed the others in order, he declared, to help draw up the *official* list of flag-raisers. Hayes protested Hansen's presence on the list; he claimed he knew for a fact that the man on the far right was Corporal Harlon Block, his and Franklin Sousley's fire-team leader and Mike Strank's assistant squad leader. On the other hand, Hayes went along with the rest of the list provided by Gagnon and confirmed by Bradley. Only then did the lieutenant colonel reveal to the three survivors that the list had just been released to the public (see Appendix C for the official April 19, 1945, list of second-flag-raisers) and was therefore a done deal, that Block and Hansen were both dead and, thus, that neither of their names should be made the focus of a controversy. He finished by *ordering* Hayes, Gagnon, and Bradley to never bring the matter up again. Later, the lieutenant colonel claimed that Hayes had not even brought the matter up during his interview.[12] Nothing that might cast negative light on the information the public received about the second flag-raising or the bond tour would be tolerated.[13]

(It is possible that the unnamed lieutenant colonel was Edward Hagenah, an experienced former newspaperman who had been installed as the deputy director of Marine Corps Public Information when that division was activated in 1942 under the aegis of Brigadier General Robert Denig, an infantryman who retired in 1940 and was called back to active service in 1942 to stand up the Marine Corps public information organization with Hagenah as his deputy, guide, and enforcer.)

Bradley

During his stay at Bethesda, waiting for his wounds to heal, Bradley agreed to participate in an interview by a U.S. Navy oral historian. The exact date of the interview is not known, but it appears to have been conducted during the slack weeks right after April 20, 1945, and before May 9. Note that there is a little confusion exhibited by John Bradley in keeping the details of the two flag-raisings separate in his memory—only weeks after the event.

Immediately after describing for the interviewer the use of an iron pipe as a staff for the first flag, Bradley hastened to add this erroneous observation: "And Joe Rosenthal happened to be there at the right time. He came up a little while after we were on top and, much to his surprise, [he took] the picture that is now so famous ... the Flag Raising on Mount Suribachi."[14] A short time later in the interview:

> **Interviewer**: Bradley, in the picture [of the second flag going up], which man are you?
> **John Bradley**: I'm the one that's second from the right as you're looking at the picture. And right next to me there you can see a man's helmet sticking up, that's Gagnon. The man bending over nearest to the ground is [Hansen]. And the one in back of us with the rifle slung on his shoulder is Ira Hayes. He is also a survivor. And the one in back of Hayes, is Sousley, who was later killed in action on the north end [of the island]. [Actually, the last man on the left is Hayes, *and* Bradley misidentified himself in the Rosenthal photo.] And there's two men that you can hardly see in the picture ... the one on the right-hand side is René Gagnon, who is a survivor of the flag raising. And the other one in back of Gagnon is Sergeant Strank, who was killed later in action on the north end of Iwo Jima.[15]

And a little later in the same interview, Bradley conflates the raising of the two flags:

Interviewer: Some naval officers that have been back [to the United States] said that the naval ships let a great cheer or salute when they noticed the flag up. Could you hear anything of that demonstration or see anything of it?

John Bradley: Well, at that time we didn't think of the significance of the flag raising, but they've told me that they did and it seems to me that I can recall something of that. We men up on top of the mountain weren't thinking of anything like that at the time. In fact we were all worried.

Interviewer: I understand this is the second flag raising that occurred there.

John Bradley: That's right. The first flag was a smaller flag and it was put up by Platoon Sergeant Ernest I. Thomas of Tallahassee, Florida .... He put up that flag about one half-hour [actually no sooner than two hours] before this larger one was put up. It was so small that it couldn't be seen from down below,[16] so our battalion commander, Lieutenant Colonel Chandler W. Johnson, sent a four-man patrol [Strank's] up with this larger flag, which is the flag you see on the poster for the 7th War [Bond] drive.[17]

By Presidential Order

By the time April 19 ended, President Harry Truman had issued a presidential order that transferred the three living second-flag-raisers from the war department to the treasury department for the duration of the 7th War Bond Drive.[18]

On April 20, less than 24 hours after Hayes flew into the nation's capital, he was scheduled to join Gagnon and Bradley for a full day of work.[19] Though the 7th War Bond tour was officially scheduled to begin on May 9, for the three heroes of Iwo Jima it had already begun.

The Tour

The 7th War Bond Drive was a new kind of combat for the largely unprepared Iwo Jima survivors freshly plucked from the bloody battlefield. For them, the bond drive effectively began at 7.30 a. m., Eastern War Time, when they arrived at the department of the treasury building to meet Secretary Henry Morganthau, Jr. The secretary, with his long-time friend, the late Franklin Roosevelt, was the driving force behind the bond drive. At least $13 billion had to be raised in a matter of a few weeks in order to pay down the debt for the prosecution of the world war. The ostensible point of the meeting was for Gagnon, Hayes, and Bradley to show Morganthau the "first" off the presses of 3.5 million posters that would emblemize the bond drive, a subtly improved full-color painting of the second flag-raising emblazoned with the powerful words, "Now, All Together" and sequestered in a gilt frame. As uplifting as the poster's debut would be to news reporters and photographers—and their readers—the real motive was to get a head start in launching the fund-raising mission with a newsworthy event.

Even more newsworthy, the second stop of the day was to be a meeting with President Harry Truman, to whom the flag-raisers would be introduced by Secretary Morganthau so they could personally present the commander-in-chief with the "first" bond-drive poster. But Morganthau's prior meeting was running long when the soon-to-be-baptized heroes arrived, so they nervously twiddled their thumbs and self-consciously fidgeted until he could receive them. In the end, they arrived at the White House on time, presented the gilt-framed poster to the President, showed him where each flag-raiser stood in the slightly adapted painting, exchanged trivialities, and were ushered out in plenty of time to leave for their third official stop of the day.[20]

The small convoy bearing the heroes and their handlers ventured straight down Pennsylvania Avenue to Capitol Hill, and there the party was shown to the doors of the Senate chamber, where their senatorial host greeted them. While the heroes waited outside, their host announced them and suggested that the august body stand in recess. As Hayes, Bradley, and Gagnon stepped across the threshold, the senators crowded around like so many puppies, all seeking handshakes and issuing plummy phrases of praise. After the rush had subsided, Speaker of the House Sam Rayburn escorted the moonstruck servicemen to a Capitol luncheon in their honor.

That evening, Speaker Rayburn took the heroes of Iwo Jima to the 1945 season's opening game between the Washington Senators and the New York Yankees at Griffith Park. The three young men in uniform, one of whom hobbled along with the aid of crutches, were led to home plate and bathed in the powerful illumination of a spotlight. As they stood stiffly at attention, an announcer introduced them, and the crowd of 24,000 fans rose to its feet to ogle and cheer them. Then they were reunited in choice box seats with Speaker Rayburn, who threw out the first ball.[21]

On the morning of May 9, 1945, the day Germany surrendered uncondi-tionally to the Allied armies in Europe and the official launch of the Mighty 7th War Bond Drive, the three heroes were driven once again to the United States Capitol, where they raised to half-staff[22] the very same flag they had raised atop Suribachi on February 23. Hayes handled the halyard, Bradley straightened the folds in the ascending flag, and Gagnon stood at rigid attention. As soon as the flag was up—its trailing edge tattered by the strong winds over Suribachi—a round of speeches was launched: Secretary of the Navy James Forrestal; Treasury Secretary Henry Morganthau, Jr.; Commandant of the Marine Corps Alexander Vandegrift; and Speaker of the House Sam

Rayburn. And as soon the last words of the last speech had faded, the Capitol Plaza, where a sales booth had been installed, was opened to mobs of gawkers and a fair number of men and women comprising the bond-buying public.[23]

On May 10, the trio of flag-raisers was joined by their newly appointed chaperone (and fixer), Technical Sergeant Keyes Beech, at Washington's Union Station for the train ride to New York's Grand Central Station. There, they were greeted by an immense crowd of well-wishers and gawkers in the Main Hall, which was festooned with giant copies of the 7th Drive's iconic poster, a theme duplicated all along the ten-block route to the famed Waldorf-Astoria Hotel, where another huge poster had been affixed over the main entrance. At this early point in the tour, the three heroes were as much gawkers as the gawkers who turned out in legions to gawk at them.[24]

They signed autographs at Times Square's Roxy Theater on Thursday, May 11, and attended a bond-selling event hosted by the ready-to-wear clothing industry that garnered $100 million in pledges. They also attended a luncheon at which life insurance executives mobilized 30,000 New York City-area insurance agents to sell war bonds.[25]

The biggest show was held on Friday, May 11, at noon, in Times Square. There, a five-story half-size replica—base to flagpole's tip—of the Felix de Weldon flag-raising statue, had been deployed under wraps on 43rd Street in front of the Bank of Manhattan for a flag-raising ceremony. As many thousands of citizens—including 50 Iwo Jima veterans being treated at local naval hospitals—looked on, the three removed the shroud and John Bradley raised Old Glory while Hayes and Gagnon, General Vandegrift, and Mayor Fiorello La Guardia saluted.[26]

As bond sales commenced around Times Square following a speech by General Vandegrift, the commandant and his trio of heroes ducked out to attend another flag-raising/bond-selling event built around another down-sized de Weldon statue. It was there that the press began to ask the heroes how they felt about their role in the public eye.[27]

It is amazing what the heady experience of only a few days on the stump churned up in three young Americans freshly home from one of the bloodiest battle endured by Marines in the Pacific. Though by no means statistically useful, the social standing Hayes, Gagnon, and Bradley brought to the discussion is nonetheless interesting: Bradley was a middle-class son of the upper Midwest, a nice, earnest young man already well along in his quest for a life-long ambition to become a mortician; Gagnon was a poor French-Canadian, held in low repute while growing up due to his ethnicity, his poverty, his fatherlessness, and many sacrifices made in order to get food on the table; Hayes was an intelligent but under-educated Native American raised on a subsistence-level farm on an isolated, poverty-stricken reservation in a part of the country where all Native Americans were treated as bothersome outsiders. Yet their reaction to their temporary turn in the national limelight brought out the same emotions in all of them.

Against the backdrop of the enormous wealth or celebrity that character-ized the most-courted segments of the bond drive's target audience, René Gagnon—who had developed high hopes of making profitable job connections on the tour—admitted in a moment of desperate guilt and boredom that he would rather return to the field of battle than sit through another high-falutin' bond-tour event, eating steak every night while his mates in Company E trained hard at isolated Camp Tarawa and dined on crap food while they prepared to invade Japan.

More than the others, John Bradley drew the line at openly agreeing with the hoopla that he was in any way a hero. When asked about his heroism in raising the second flag, he said it was just a replacement for the first flag (which he had helped to raise), and that every man on Iwo Jima and aboard ship around it on February 23 had played an essential role in getting the flag up and ultimately securing the island.

It was duly noted that all three living second-flag-raisers, Bradley more than Gagnon and Hayes, looked sour and ill-at-ease when questioned about their feelings and deeds.

Hayes, always a dutiful, squared-away, unimpaired Marine in the field, qui-etly resorted to the bottle under the unfamiliar, unnatural, overwhelming stress he experienced while out in bond-tour world. In this he was apparently abetted by the worldly-wise Technical Sergeant Beech, a hard-bitten, hard-drinking foreign-correspondent type of newsman who mentored Hayes, got him to events on time, and helped him drown his sorrows and discomfort in liquor. Very quickly under this regime, Hayes's canned speech came to consist of one sentence of miserable platitudes, or just a huge yawn. When not actually the center of attention, Hayes had a marked tendency to nod off until he heard his name spoken aloud.[28]

The rising tension simmered through stops in Philadelphia and Boston (where 200,000 onlookers turned out in a driving rain storm), then it was back to New York for an emotional reprise on Wall Street at which the mothers of Mike Strank, Franklin Sousley, and Hank Hansen were trotted out to meet the three survivors for the first time. All the heroes and moms choked, were unable to look one another in the eye, had to avert their eyes in the presence of more outsized posters featuring the Rosenthal flag-raising shot. No words were shared either. Everyone in viewing distance choked up.

The course from Wall Street was set: stops in Rochester, Cleveland, Akron, Canton, Detroit, and Indianapolis. By then, the only thing holding Hayes together was the excitement of drawing closer to his home in Arizona for a scheduled rally in Phoenix. But it was not to be. The anger and embarrassment that had been building from the first day onward bubbled to the surface in Chicago.[29]

Gagnon's main issue had become the fact that Hayes was always surrounded by well-wishers when photographers and newsmen were around but shunned by the same well-wishers after prying eyes were escorted from the scene.

Bradley's strongest issue resolved itself in the form of increasingly anger-tinged remarks to onlookers and the press that many of the civilians who turned out to see the show avoided the purchase of war bonds.[30]

Hayes avoided the appearance of anger and resentment by turning up for each appearance playing the affable drunk, but he disappeared from a Chicago theater when he was supposed to be lined up with Gagnon and Bradley to kiss an A-list actress in public. The next morning, as the bond troupe prepared for an early appearance at Soldier Field, the police arrived to inform the heroes' handlers that Hayes, who was with them, had been picked up during the night for disturbing the peace in a Loop bar.

Beech managed to get Hayes to Soldier Field, but he was accosted by General Vandegrift following the troupe's showy entrance. The commandant asked Technical Sergeant Beech if it was true that Hayes had gotten drunk the previous night. Beech admitted it was true. Then Vandegrift asked how much more time was left on the tour. Beech said a month remained. The general, who was just back from a tour of Iwo Jima, where his battalion-commander son had been wounded, muttered, "My god. My god."[31]

That evening, a public information officer dispatched from Headquarters, Marine Corps, arrived in Chicago and went straight to Hayes to hand him an airline ticket and tell him that his services were no longer required, that he was to head straight back to Hawaii by air—no stops along the way. Beech attempted to dissuade the officer but was rebuffed: this was an iron-clad order passed down from the highest command authority. And, no, there would be no family reunion in Arizona; Private First Class Hayes was ordered to stay away from Phoenix. Hayes's flight left on time at 9 p. m. and Hayes was on it. The next morning, the handlers announced that Hayes had demanded to return to Company E to train for the invasion of Japan, a demand that the Marine Corps was happy to give in to.[32]

Hayes later summed it up in a letter: "I was sick. I guess I was about to crack, thinking of the guys who were better men than me not coming back at all, much less to the White House. On the reservation I got hundreds of letters and I got sick of hearing about the flag raising and sometimes I wished that guy had never made the picture."[33]

For Gagnon and Bradley, the ordeal lasted through July 4. Bradley hated every minute of it, and so did Beech. Gagnon got used to it even as he waited in vain for a benefactor to hire or recommend him for a job. The cities they visited after Chicago stretched by way of northern and central rail routes all the way to the Pacific Northwest, turned south along the coast, then swung back to the East via central and southern rail routes. It was a grind.

The Mighty 7th War Bond Tour ended where it had begun, at a fireworks display in Washington, D.C. A final tally, made public at the end of the summer, revealed that the tour's $13-billion goal was exceeded by $13.3 billion—more than $26.3 billion in all (equivalent to $364 billion in 2018)—more than double the goal and more than half of the Federal budget for the year.[34]

Fame

Fame would endure, but fame for these three young men would never be as intense as it was during the bond tour. Fame would be with the three living second-flag-raisers for the rest of their lives. It offered dreams of wealth or popularity, or even a simple job, if one wanted to go that far. Dreams, though, not reality. The fame certainly feasted on the guilt of survivalhood; all three were socially impaired by the certainty that all the fame was unearned or the province of better men who had proceeded from Suribachi to early deaths on Iwo Jima. All three survivors felt jinxed by their fame yet none could really talk about it with either of the others; they were not, after all, really friends. Each came away from the experience without strong friendships with anyone. All three coped with the damning symptoms of war neurosis … whatever it was called at one time or another: post-traumatic stress disorder. None was ever free to be whom he might have been without the war, without the fame. That's the price they paid for the adulation.

CHAPTER 10

Block

1945–1947: Correcting the Record

Ada "Belle" Block—Corporal Harlon Block's mother—first saw The Photo in her local newspaper on February 25, 1945, only a few days after it was taken by Joe Rosenthal. It required only a glance to force an involuntary exclamation from Mrs. Block. She pointed at the Marine on the far right, who was seen only from behind, and blurted out, "That's Harlon," and "[I've] changed so many diapers on that boy's butt. I know it's my boy."[1]

> ## Block
>
> Corporal Harlon Block, an assistant squad leader and fire team leader in the 2nd Platoon of Company E, 28th Marines, was born on November 6, 1924, in Yorktown, Texas, and moved to Weslaco, Texas, in the Rio Grande valley, where his father sought better opportunities as a dairy farmer. An outgoing natural athlete, Block excelled at football and was named All South Texas End during his senior year of high school. He and seven school friends decided to enlist together in the Marine Corps and were honored with an early graduation in January 1943 to help them along. By April 1943, Private Block graduated from boot camp in San Diego, and on April 19, he began the course at the Parachute Training School at Camp Gillespie, California, from which he graduated with a promotion to private first class. He was shipped to New Caledonia in the South Pacific Area and served in the 1st Marine Parachute Regiment headquarters. First combat was experienced in December 1943 while Block was serving with Weapons Company, 1st Marine Parachute Battalion. Upon return to the United States when the paramarine program was terminated in February 1944, Block was ordered to Company E, 28th Marines. He was promoted corporal and assistant squad leader on October 27, 1944.[2]

Harlon Block, who had been a member of the 2nd Platoon's four-man wire team on February 23, 1945, could not bolster his mother's claim that he appears in the Rosenthal flag-raising photo; he had been killed in action by a Japanese mortar round on March 1, 1945, only hours after rising to lead his squad following the death of Sergeant Mike Strank.

On April 7, 1945, in Washington, D.C., Private First Class René Gagnon once again misidentified Block's image, reporting that it was the 3rd Platoon's Sergeant Hank Hansen's. This error was compounded on April 19 by an official Marine Corps press release that named six men as second-flag-raisers: Sergeant Mike Strank, Sergeant Hank Hansen, Pharmacist's Mate John Bradley, Private First Class Ira Hayes, Private First Class Franklin Sousley, and Private First Class René Gagnon. (See Appendix C.) And then compounded again when Doc Bradley agreed with all of Gagnon's identifications—including his own.

(It is not known which, if any, photographs, other than Joe Rosenthal's, were available to Gagnon, Hayes, and Bradley during their Washington sojourn. Staff Sergeant Lou Lowery's and Private Bob Campbell's film took a long, long time to reach a photo lab in the United States.)

The official yarn that involved Block being swapped out and Hansen being swapped in as a matter of convenience—preyed on Ira Hayes's sense of fairness. A man who kept his own counsel for as long as doing so was practical, Hayes had yet to tell anyone that the figure of the right-most second-flag-raiser could not possibly have been Hansen. Of all the former paramarines on the volcano when Joe Rosenthal released his camera shutter, Hayes was reasonably certain that only Hansen was wearing calf-high, brown leather paramarine jump boots.[3] Hayes also knew that Block wore standard issue ankle-high, sueded-pigskin Marine boondockers. That day, Hayes had seen—and many February 23 Suribachi photographs clearly showed—Hansen in his paramarine jump boots. As well, Hayes had climbed the volcano alongside Block as a member of Block's own three-man fire team, which with Mike Strank constituted the four-man wire team assigned to run a field telephone line through to Lieutenant Schrier. As observant a Marine as Hayes was, it is very likely that he had noticed that his fellow paramarine—and close friend—was wearing boondockers during and after the ascent on Suribachi.

When he was honorably discharged from the Marine Corps—a corporal and a proud veteran—on December 1, 1945, Hayes decided to confront the matter head-on. It took him seven months to move the ball, and he did not do so until he first received a letter from Belle Block.

At first, Hayes was content to post a letter to Block's mother, just to tell her that he knew for a certainty that Hank Hansen was not and Harlon was definitely the flag-raiser nearest to the base of the flagpole when the Rosenthal photo was taken.

> July 12, 1946
>
> Dear Mrs. Block,
>
> I got your letter just recently and God knows how happy I was to get your letter.
>
> I have prayed & waited for such a happening as this. I was kinda worried to make the first move.
>
> I knew your son very well & was with him at the time he was killed. And you can well be proud of him for he died a good Marine & very outstanding on the battlefield. I'm writing this cause I was there & I know & saw.
>
> Harlon was in on this picture. But how they fouled up the picture I don't know. I have Bradley to back me up on this & another score of men in our old company.
>
> I was the last man to come back to the States for this big bond drive. I tried my darndest to stay overseas, but couldn't, all because they had a man in there [i.e., Hansen] that really wasn't, & besides that had Sousley and myself switched around [in the flag photo and caption]. And when I arrived in Washington, D.C., I tried to set the thing right, but some colonel told me to not say another word as the two men were dead, meaning Harlon and Hansen. And besides, the public knew who was who in the picture at the time & I didn't want no last-minute commotion. Well, all this error prompted me to go back to my old outfit after 2 weeks on the bond drive & still had a month & a half to go. And naturally, by all means, it did not seem right for such a brave Marine as your son not to get any national recognition …
>
> There may be lots of accusations towards me for not letting this out any sooner. But I was just bidding [sic] for time in hearing from you. But now that you have done so, I am happy at last we can get this thing settled. You have Bradley and myself to back you up in letting this error known.
>
> As I said before, Block was a swell guy, always a lot of fun, a favorite with everyone. When he was killed, he never knew what hit him.
>
> The last day on the island we had memorial services for the boys. I was hurt and sick. I found Block, Strank & Sousley's grave[s] & offered each a little prayer. We hit Iwo Jima with 250 men & only 27 of us came back, & it was made possible by the sacrifice of your dear son & others, & we will make the best of anything & will never forget.[4]

The letter was appreciated, but it failed to rouse the Block family to action. So, on some long-forgotten date in July or August 1946, Hayes left the Gila River Indian Community in Arizona to undertake the 1,300-mile trek to Weslaco, Texas, to come clean in person before Harlon Block's parents.

Hayes's arrival at the Block farm was greeted with authentic warmth as the former paramarine got down to the business at hand: he told Harlon's father, Edward, that Harlon was absolutely in the Rosenthal photo, at the extreme right, securing the base of the heavy iron flagpole. (This was the same figure that Belle Block had reflexively identified as Harlon the very first time she saw The Photo in her local newspaper.)

In short order, after Hayes left to return to Arizona, Mrs. Block went to work to persuade Edward to send a letter to their local congressman to ask that he request an official inquiry into the matter. The letter was sent in September 1946 and was answered in very short order by Lieutenant Colonel Edward Hagenah, who wrote that he worked for General Vandegrift, the commandant of the Marine Corps. Hagenah agreed to investigate all of the men credited with taking part in the second flag-raising.[5] Ira Hayes's testimony, including his earlier efforts to right the wrong, went a long way toward helping Harlon Block's cause. Having been warned in April 1945—possibly by Lieutenant Colonel Hagenah himself—of dire consequences if they strayed from the official line, Gagnon and Bradley both nonetheless allowed that the right-most flag-raiser "could be Block." Nothing bad happened.

It took only a month for an outcome to emerge: in January 1947, the Marine Corps officially dropped Hansen from the roster of second-flag-raisers (he remained officially—and accurately—recognized as a *first*-flag-raiser). The investigators magnanimously allowed that no blame would be leveled for the error of affixing the wrong name to Block's image.[6]

So, it was official: the six second-flag-raisers were now identified as Strank, Block, Hayes, Sousley, Gagnon, and Bradley. It was a line-up that endured until mid-2016.

What Became of Them

What became of the principal players after the flag-raising?

René Gagnon was transferred from the 5th Marine Division to the 6th in July 1945 for occupation duty in China. He was married before he went back overseas in September 1945. Following a five-month tour of duty, he was ordered back to the United States, where he arrived on April 20, 1946, and was separated from the Marine Corps with the rank of corporal on April 27. There ensued more than three decades of frustration owing to highly touted recognition and whispers of job offers during and after the war-bond tour, offers that never came through. Once the bond drive was concluded on July 4, 1945, all the hero worship by public figures came to an abrupt end. Gagnon was briefly in the public eye during the November 1954 ceremonies attending the dedication of Felix de Weldon's Marine Corps War Memorial, and he traveled to Iwo Jima in February 1965 for invasion anniversary ceremonies. He even attended a few 5th Marine Division Association reunions at the urging of his wife, but he appeared to lose interest in his fame and seems to have preferred a simple life lived in obscurity. From all appearances, he simply drifted along until October 12, 1979, when he suffered a fatal heart attack in the boiler room of an apartment complex for which he was maintenance director. He was initially interred in a Manchester, New Hampshire, Catholic cemetery but was moved to Arlington National Cemetery in 1981.[1]

Ira Hayes tried very hard to live in humble obscurity following the traumatic Mighty 7th War Bond tour and his successful intervention into correcting the record about Harlon Block's participation in the second-flag-raising. But as much as he craved obscurity, too many days at the isolated Gila River Indian Community were punctuated by visits from strangers who just wanted to bask in the warmth of his fame. He was cordial to these strangers, but he disliked the show he felt compelled to put on. He bolstered himself with drink and spiraled downward. In 1949, he appeared briefly with John Wayne in *Sands of Iwo Jima*, in which he hands the actual second flag to René Gagnon. Nevertheless, Hayes could not hold onto a job for months at a stretch, and he was arrested 52 times around the country for public drunkenness or other alcohol-related transgressions. His humiliation during a 1953 trip to Chicago illustrates his travail. Police picked him up on the city's skid row, drunk, in torn clothing, penniless, and shoeless. He was remanded to the House of Correction until the Chicago *Sun-Times* newspaper learned of his arrest, paid his fine, and set up a public fund to get him home to Arizona.[2]

For all that, Hayes managed to remain sober throughout the ceremonies attending the dedication of the Marine Corps War Memorial on November 10, 1954. His pride as a Marine never wavered even though he cringed when President Dwight Eisenhower referred to him as a hero.

He lasted about three months after his war memorial appearance. He was found dead from alcohol poisoning on the morning of January 24, 1955, following an evening of drinking and card-playing in an abandoned hut near his birthplace in Sacaton. The official story declares that another man, also drunk, wanted to settle a score with Hayes, and the uninvolved men in the hut left him and Hayes to it. No one knows what happened, but the condition of Ira Hayes's corpse is said to have suggested foul play. There was no autopsy and the police declined to launch an investigation. (Another story, as told in the *New York Times* issue of January 25, 1955,[3] is that Hayes stepped out of the abandoned building after drinking a half-gallon of muscatel, never returned, and was found face-down the next morning, drowned in a puddle of vomit.)

Ira Hayes was buried—and lauded again as a hero—at Arlington National Cemetery on February 2, 1955. René Gagnon and John Bradley both attended the interment and spoke at the graveside ceremony.

It appears from the record of Ira Hayes's post-war decline that his very first instinct aboard ship bound for Camp Tarawa, when René Gagnon first came acalling—avoid fame—would have been the correct instinct for him to follow.

Ray Jacobs was mustered out of the Marine Corps in 1946 and went to work for KTVU in Oakland, California, first as a reporter, then as a news anchor, and finally as the news director. He sometimes ran into Joe Rosenthal and Bob Campbell, who were working as staff photographers for the *San Francisco Chronicle*. Jacobs, a Marine Corps reservist, was called up in 1950 for the Korean War. He served for a year in California as an instructor and was honorably discharged. He retired from KTVU in 1992 and spent his later years amassing proof to support—and ultimately win approval for—his claim to have been the "unknown radioman" seen in many photos taken on

Suribachi's summit. Jacobs closed the eyewitness account of his adventures atop Suribachi thusly: "It was close to noon when I received the word that I was relieved and should return to my unit, F Company. I reported to Lieutenant Schrier, then started the long slip and slide down the steep flank of Suribachi."

Then the crux of the dilemma Jacobs faced to make his claim stick: "I had been with Schrier's E Company patrol for just over two hours and now I was leaving it as abruptly as I had joined it. It's ironic that for this one brief noteworthy moment in Marine Corps history we had worked so closely together and yet I didn't know any of the members of the patrol, and they didn't know me."[4]

Ray Jacobs passed away in Redding, California, on January 29, 2008, aged 82 years.

Chuck Lindberg was wounded in the forearm while attacking a Japanese mortar position on March 1, 1945. He was eventually evacuated to Saipan and was there for two weeks before he saw the Rosenthal flag-raising photo for the first time. "I looked at it," he later reported, "and I said, 'That's not ours. That's not the way we did it.' I couldn't figure out what happened." Lindberg was moved to a hospital in Hawaii and recalled being there for about three weeks before a copy of the March 30, 1945, edition of *Yank* magazine fell into his hands. The Rosenthal flag-raising photo was featured. "That's the first I knew exactly what happened." Lou Lowery had made it back to the *Leatherneck* magazine offices in Washington, D.C., and had developed his film of the first flag-raising. "He must have taken the slow boat," Lindberg quipped.

The former Raider and flamethrower operator was released from medical care and ordered to the naval brig in Charleston, South Carolina, to complete his four-year hitch as a guard. After receiving a Silver Star medal for his tour on Iwo Jima, Lindberg mustered out of the Marine Corps in early 1946 and made a beeline to the *Leatherneck* offices to see Lou Lowery, now the magazine's photo editor. Lowery gave Lindberg more photos and told him what he could about how the second flag and its flag-raisers had taken precedence over the first—to the point that hardly any Americans remembered the first flag at all.

Chuck Lindberg returned home to Grand Forks, North Dakota, got married, and settled in Richfield, Minnesota, to raise his five children. He worked as an electrician. It wasn't until the 1970s that he began to make himself available, mostly at schools, to discuss his role and his feelings about the flag-raising issue. He attended the dedication of the Iwo Jima memorial statue on November 10, 1954, but went unrecognized by the many influential speakers.[5] Hardly anyone believed his story at first, but more and more details reached the public consciousness until, by the time he flew to Iwo Jima to celebrate the 50th anniversary of both flag-raisings in 1995, the story was pretty much accepted by the relatively few Americans who cared enough to listen.

Speaking in front of a 5th Marine Division reunion crowd in the late 1990s, Chuck Lindberg revealed a softening of his position on the recognition of the raisers of both flags: "I have always felt it was a mistake to identify the Marines that raised the flag on Iwo Jima. Every man that went ashore at Iwo, and every man at sea, raised the flag—every one [of us]. We carried it up there, and we had our hands on the pole, but every one of you raised it, and most of all, the men who didn't come back—they all raised it."[6]

Lindberg attended the last reunion of Company E's 3rd Platoon in 2007 and passed away in Edina, Minnesota, on June 29 of that year. He was memorialized in speeches and honored with a flyover by military jets and vintage propeller-driven warplanes. Of all the flag-raisers, Chuck Lindberg was the last to go.[7]

Corporal Charles W. Lindberg, USMC
Silver Star Citation:
For conspicuous gallantry and intrepidity while serving as Flame Thrower Operator of Company E, Second Battalion, Twenty-Eight Marines, Fifth Marine Division, in action against enemy Japanese forces on Iwo Jima, Volcano Islands, from 19 February to 1 March 1945. Repeatedly exposing himself to hostile grenades and machine-gun fire in order that he might reach and neutralize enemy pill-boxes at the base of Mount Suribachi, Corporal Lindberg courageously approached within ten or fifteen yards of the emplacements before discharging his weapon, thereby assuring annihilation of the enemy and the successful completion of his platoon's mission. As a member of the first combat patrol to scale Mount Suribachi, he courageously carried his flame thrower to the steep slopes and assisted in destroying the occupants of the many caves found in the rim of the volcano, some of which contained as many as seventy Japanese. While engaged in an attack on hostile cave positions on March 1, he fearlessly exposed himself to accurate enemy fire and was subsequently wounded and evacuated. By his determinations in manning his weapon, despite its weight and the extreme heat developed in operation, Corporal Lindberg greatly assisted in securing his company's position. His courage and devotion to duty were in keeping with the highest traditions of the United States Naval Service.

Lou Lowery remained on the *Leatherneck* staff as photo editor until 1976, when he was named the Marine Corps Association photo director, a position from which he retired in 1982. He also remained in the Marine Corps Reserve, from which he retired with rank of captain. And he was a founder and active member of the Marine Corps Combat Correspondents' Association.

Lowery and Joe Rosenthal ultimately became close friends. Rosenthal once explained to an interviewer: "There may have been some doubt about which of us was the better photographer, but there was no doubt about who was luckier."

Lou Lowery passed away on April 15, 1987, at the age of seventy. Flying in to attend his funeral were Joe Rosenthal and Chuck Lindberg.[8]

Joe Rosenthal was awarded the 1945 Pulitzer Prize for photography. He quit his job at the Associated Press in late 1945 and joined Times Wide World Photos as manager and chief photographer, but he ultimately settled in at the *San Francisco Chronicle,* where he worked as a simple—but always notable—photographer until taking retirement in 1981. While at the *Chronicle,* he worked with former private Bob Campbell and ran into Ray Jacobs, the Company F radioman, who worked as a broadcast journalist in Oakland, California. Joe's name was inscribed on the Marine Corps War Memorial in 1983, and on April 13, 1996, he was named an honorary Marine by the commandant of the Marine Corps. Joe Rosenthal passed away on August 20, 2006, in Novato, California, aged 94, and is interred in San Francisco.[9] He was posthumously awarded the Department of the Navy Distinguished Public Service Award with this citation:

> For exceptionally distinguished public service in support of the United States Navy and Marine Corps. On February 23, 1945, a bespectacled Mr. Rosenthal made a picture of five U.S. Marines and one U.S. Navy corpsman that immortalized the American Fighting spirit during World War II and became an everlasting symbol of service and sacrifice, transcending art and the ages. Mr. Rosenthal's poor eyesight prohibited him from serving in the armed services, so, he instead went to war summoning the craft he had practiced since the Great Depression. He bravely accompanied island-hopping forces in the Pacific as a civilian news photographer. On Iwo Jima, Japan, short of breath from climbing the 546-foot volcano, Mr. Rosenthal, in haste, stood on top of shaky rocks in search of the best graphic composition. As the six men hoisted an iron pole and the American flag unfurled in a smart breeze for all to see, Mr. Rosenthal captured the precise moment, unaware, until much later, of its significance. Since that very day, his iconic photo has stood as a testament to the perseverance, esprit and dedication of American Marines. In recognition of his own service and dedication, Mr. Rosenthal is posthumously awarded the Department of the Navy Distinguished Public Service Award.

Harold George Schrier was assigned to command Company D, 28th Marines, for the second half of the Iwo Jima campaign and departed Iwo Jima for Hawaii with the 5th Marine Division immediately following the end of the bloody fighting. He worked in the San Diego area beginning in mid-1945, then served in the Far East until 1949, when he was assigned as technical advisor on the John Wayne movie *Sands of Iwo Jima,* in which he also played himself. When war broke out in Korea on June 25, 1950, Captain Schrier was rushed to South Korea as a member of the 1st Marine Brigade. He served as brigade adjutant in the Pusan Perimeter and the Inchon invasion, after which the 1st Marine Brigade was fully merged into the 1st Marine Division. Schrier was given command of an infantry company early in the Chosin Reservoir campaign and was wounded in the neck while commanding the defense of a vital hilltop position. He was evacuated to Japan, promoted to major, and undertook recruiting duty in Birmingham, Alabama, until reassigned to the Marine Corps Recruit Depot staff. He retired as a lieutenant colonel in 1957 and died in Bradenton, Florida, in 1971.[10]

> First Lieutenant Harold G. Schrier, USMC
>   Navy Cross Citation:
>   For extraordinary heroism as Executive Officer of Company E, Second Battalion, Twenty-Eighth Marines, Fifth Marine Division, in action against enemy Japanese forces on Iwo Jima, Volcano Islands, on 23 February 1945. On the morning of 23 February when his combat team had advanced to the base of Mount Suribachi after four days of severe fighting, First Lieutenant Schrier volunteered to lead a forty-man patrol up the steep slopes of the mountain. Quickly organizing his patrol and placing himself at its head, he began the tortuous climb up the side of the volcano, followed by his patrol in single file. Employing the only known approach, an old Japanese trail, he swiftly pushed on until, covered by all the supporting weapons of his battalion, he gained the top of the mountain despite hostile small arms and artillery fire. Forced to engage the remaining enemy in a sharp fire fight, he overcame them without loss in his patrol and occupied the rim of the volcano. Although still under enemy sniper fire, First Lieutenant Schrier, assisted by his Platoon Sergeant, raised the National Colors over Mount Suribachi, planting the flagstaff firmly on the highest knoll overlooking the crater, the first American flag to fly over any land in the inner defenses of the Japanese Empire. His inspiring leadership, courage and determination in the face of overwhelming odds upheld the highest traditions of the United States Naval Service.

Dave Severance was detached from the 5th Marine Division shortly after reaching Camp Tarawa, Hawaii, from Iwo Jima; he had been given an opportunity to attend flight school, which he had naïvely thought was the agreement he had worked out with his Marine Corps recruiter in 1938. He earned his wings in due course and flew night fighters in combat during the Korean War. Severance retired from the Marine Corps as a colonel in 1968 and thereafter volunteered his time to various Marine Corps veterans' groups. He currently lives in La Jolla, California, one of the very few living Iwo Jima veterans.[11]

Phil Ward, a proud son of Crawfordsville, Indiana, and a member of the Assault Squad of Company E's 3rd Platoon, was two weeks shy of his 19th birthday when he stormed ashore onto Iwo Jima's Beach Green. Photos available within days of February 23, 1945, prove he was hands-on during the launch of the first flag, but he was never officially acknowledged during his lifetime.[12] He was one of only four original 3rd Platoon men who was not wounded or killed in action on Iwo. A lifelong resident of Crawfordsville, 79-year-old Phil Ward passed away in a hospital near his McAllen, Texas, winter home on December 28, 2002. He is interred in Arlington National Cemetery.[13]

George Greeley Wells remained on active duty in the Marine Corps until his retirement as a captain in November 1957. Thereafter, he had a successful and fulfilling career in business. Always conscious of giving back to his community, Wells served on his local city council and planning commission, then in stints as mayor and police commissioner. Following his full retirement in the early 2000s, Greeley and his wife moved from New Jersey to Washington State to be near their daughter. He spent as much time as he could supporting the Marine Corps and spending time with local Marines. Greeley Wells passed away on September 22, 2014.[14]

Keith Wells remained on Iwo Jima for the duration of the battle, but he did not return to combat owing to his wounds. He returned to Texas A&M after the war and earned his degree in petroleum geology in 1948. Wells retired from the Marine Corps Reserve in 1959 with the rank of major and wrote a war memoir, *Give Me 50 Marines Not Afraid to Die: Iwo Jima.* John Keith Wells died on February 11, 2016, aged ninety-four.[15]

CHAPTER 12

The Irishman and the Omahan

The only thing needed to free the brain to notice something no one else has noticed is freeing oneself from the illusion it should have been noticed by someone else before now.

He had the time; he could afford the obsession.

Stephen Foley, a Wexford, Ireland, building supply worker, had been interested in—some say obsessed with—World War II in the Pacific since he was a teenager. Over time, his interest honed in on the bloody battle for Iwo Jima.

In the late summer of 2013, Foley was forced to stay home for four weeks of inactivity to heal from a hernia operation, and he thought he might use the forced rest to study up on his favorite topic. He would read through a pile of Iwo Jima books he had never had in hand before, looking for new information.

It was no time before Foley selected a book with the universally familiar Joe Rosenthal flag-raising photo on the cover; the book was filled with high-quality photos of the flag-raising scene that were new to Foley. But something didn't seem right: photos of U.S. Navy hospital corpsman John Bradley that Foley found in the book did not seem to match the image of Bradley found on the cover, in the Rosenthal photo. Certain aspects of his clothing and carried equipment, or maybe details of his face, just seemed to be, well, a little different.

Foley had a computer. He knew where the Iwo Jima websites were; he was a member of the Iwo Jima amateur historians' community. And he had weeks of time to kill. Hmm. What if ... he took the time he had to minutely study the high-resolution photos available on his computer, look most carefully at items of clothing and equipment Bradley appeared to be wearing or carrying in many—but not all—of the photos in which he had been captioned. Maybe then Stephen Foley could get some rest from his burgeoning obsession with John Bradley.

As the days progressed and the apparent anomalies piled up, Foley had to start a detailed list to keep the two figures captioned "Bradley" straight in his mind. Foley eventually became convinced he was tracking two men who looked a lot alike in the photos but wore different clothing and equipment. For example, one "Bradley"—eventually dubbed "Mystery Man" for lack of a real name—wore a soft cover between his helmet and his scalp while the other was bareheaded beneath his steel pot helmet. One carried medical aid bags. The other did not. One—the same one who wore the soft cover but no medical bags—had on an ammunition belt built to take the loaded eight-round M1 rifle clips. He was doubtless a combatant. The other, who did sport medical aid bags worn at belt height, also wore a belt built for magazines for a.45-caliber pistol. He was armed the way a corpsman—or officer—would be, more indicative of how the "real" Bradley was equipped than a rifleman. And so forth. Once Foley cracked these clues, he realized he was on the way to denying the hospital corpsman his place as a flag-raiser.

From these beginnings, Stephen Foley fashioned an airtight case that proved Bradley could not have had a hand in raising the second flag—because he wore or didn't wear certain articles of equipment or clothing. *Someone* had been the sixth man, but it was not Bradley. And so, by countless more repeated glances between details of many photos, Foley worked out the fact that, at the very least, the previously acknowledged position of one of the actual flag-raisers—Franklin Sousley—had to be moved one place forward to accommodate the emergent facts gleaned from the fevered study of photos. And a new, unknown, flag-raiser—Mystery Man—whose spot *had been* covered had to be identified to replace Bradley.

And that was when Stephen Foley was cleared to return to work. He already knew that he would have to turn his exhaustive evidence over to someone better able to make the case among amateur military historians *and* professional military historians, especially those living in the United States. As it happened, Foley had that person in mind.

Until Stephen Foley terminated his frenetic four-week photo analysis to return to his life, it seemed that only two other men on Earth had known that the long-acknowledged flag-raiser did not in fact help to raise the second flag. One was the long-acknowledged flag-raiser himself—Bradley—a man who appeared to have accepted the honor passively and apparently never uttered a word on the subject. The other was Mystery Man, who had somehow had his photo taken and released to a huge swathe of humanity without ever being noticed or identified.

The Omahan

Eric Krelle, a resident of Omaha, U.S. Marines buff, World War II reenacter, and father of three, earns a living as a toy designer while spending his spare time administering a popular World War II website, 5thMarineDivision.com The site is considered authoritative on the topics of the division's role at Iwo Jima and its brief and incomplete foray into the Vietnam War.

It was Krelle who stepped up when Stephen Foley had to go back to work at the end of four weeks of surgical leave. It was Krelle who would be first to test Foley's photography-based theories regarding John Bradley's presence on the second Suribachi flag-raising team. *And* it would be Krelle who would take the first crack at discovering who the new sixth second-flag-raiser might be.

First thing, Krelle went to work covering Foley's labors with photos and film, to be sure Foley had seen what was really there and that his work could be duplicated at will. All the relevant photos and film footage were nailed down by way of exhaustive study.

His own repeated exposure of the film and his fresh eye made it possible for Krelle to notice a few things Foley had missed. One such was seen only when, in one batch of film, the chief candidate—"Mystery Man"—approached the camera and briefly exposed the left side of his head. Right there, with barely time to see it, is something that ultimately resolved itself after countless viewings as a short strap that dangled from the left side of Mystery Man's helmet, right over his left eye.

The success of Krelle's identification task would come down to what turned out to be a little snap designed to hold the unidentified flag-raiser candidate's plastic helmet liner snugly inside his steel pot. It happened that Eric Krelle's collection of World War II-era Marine Corps helmets was pivotal. Once he realized what he had found, he brought out a Marine World War II helmet and located the left liner strap.

Further, after checking every helmet on Suribachi that was captured in a photograph he could access, Krelle determined that only one helmet had a loose liner strap, period, and that it belonged to Mystery Man. Altogether, it appeared in at least a dozen still photos and printed film frames. The fact that the errant strap was associated with just one Marine was bolstered by other small details of dress and equipage logged by either or both Stephen Foley and Eric Krelle.

Armed with what he believed to be incontrovertible evidence, Krelle went to his photo archive and searched it again until he found a skinny man with a long nose who had a liner strap dangling off the left side of his helmet. The photo was Joe Rosenthal's Gung Ho photo and a hand-written caption said the man was "Pfc Harold H. Schultz." This was the first solid connection he had ever achieved with respect to raising the second flag.

With that, Krelle turned his attention to a blog post he would write to take his and Foley's detective work public and maybe earn some corroboration from professional historians, or at least a few amateur volunteers willing to duplicate the work of discovery.

And nothing happened. *Nothing.* There were no takers.

With that, Eric Krelle decided to contact the press to see if he could find a reporter interested enough to listen to his theory, a reporter who might see what he had been seeing for most of a year of mind-numbing photo research.

The plan immediately bore fruit. Krelle's luck turned around pretty much from the moment he stopped by unannounced at the *Omaha World Herald* newspaper offices and asked to speak with columnist Matthew Hansen. It was with great reluctance that Hansen made time on the spot to drink coffee with Krelle while Krelle went on and on about his and Stephen Foley's discovery. At length, Hansen found himself buying into the story. Eventually, he agreed to present the story and supporting evidence to military history authors and scholars who lived in the Omaha area.

It took a while before open hostility turned to reluctant interest, then longer before even one acknowledged expert allowed as he *might* "buy it"—before he added, "Don't quote me on that."[1] Then there were those experts who found the evidence compelling but refused to say so in public.

And then Krelle and Hansen ran across a young documentary filmmaker, Dustin Spence, who had written a *Leatherneck* magazine article in 2006 about the "mysteries" of the first flag-raising. At first, Spence showed his skeptical side. He told Eric Krelle that he was not convinced, that the differences between Bradley's dress in various photos could be explained away, that there was still too much accepted history to overcome, too many plausible explanations for naysayers to bring to bear.

This was not, in the end, skepticism; it turned out to be friendly advice: prepare a better defense of your arguments.

Slowly, the line drawn against Foley's and Krelle's research and conclusions began to bend. Two Creighton University historians, skeptical at best going in, slowly warmed to an Eric Krelle private lecture, then offered some terrific advice: they wanted to know more about Mystery Man, Harold Schultz, before offering their blessing.

That was the pivotal question: *Who was Harold Schultz?*

And then Matthew Hansen, who had been drawn into the research effort on Schultz, had a breakthrough. His mail one day included an express package from Los Angeles that had been sent by Dezreen MacDowell, who wrote in her cover letter that she was *the* Harold H. Schultz's stepdaughter and that she had been following the progress of the investigation into the identity of the new sixth second-flag-raiser.

On November 23, 2014, Matthew Hansen's article, "New Mystery Arises from Iconic Iwo Jima Image: History buff's analysis of the famous World War II photo challenges long-assumed truth," was published in the *Omaha World Herald* (http://dataomaha.com/media/news/2014/iwo-jima/). It was a lengthy look at Stephen Foley's and Eric Krelle's amateur research project, which was poised to turn long-accepted Iwo Jima battle history on its head.

In due course, thanks to opportunities that opened up in the wake of Matthew Hansen's dogged journalistic efforts, Eric Krelle began to change minds and turn his losing arguments into solid victories that spread far beyond Omaha as historians and journalists increasingly embraced—or at least openly debated—the data Foley and Krelle had painstakingly stacked up.[2]

Schultz

No living person has a useful clue pertaining to *why* Harold Schultz hid himself and his role in the second flag-raising from public view for the last half-century of his life. Speculation runs to the argument that he was a strange sort of man who marched to the beat of his own drum. Clearly (so far) Schultz eschewed the public eye and its inevitable notoriety. Perhaps he was simply shy or modest, or maybe just content with the way things worked out. They all seem like good guesses, given what little we know about Schultz from the gleanings of a massive search for at least clues about his life from 1945 to his death in 1995. Good guess, but still only guesses.

Another guess is that Schultz spent the last 50 years of his life responding to a common urge among combat veterans to compartmentalize and bury all thought of war's many traumas, to never bring it up or rise to the bait of questions posed by the uninitiated. That's another good guess, but still just a guess.

Here is the little we do know:

Harold Henry Schultz, who was born in Detroit on January 28, 1926, lived in that city until he lied about his age to enlist in the Marine Corps Reserve on December 23, 1943. He was ultimately assigned to the crew-served weapons platoon in Company E, 2nd Battalion, 28th Marines.

Private First Class Schultz was attached to the Schrier patrol on February 23, 1945, and, by all modern accounts, provided close-in security for the first flag when it was raised. (See Photos D and E.) He and René Gagnon were bystanders when they were called upon by Mike Strank at the last moment to lend a hand lifting the large second flag, which was affixed to an iron flagpole too heavy for four men—Strank and Block's three-man fire team—to get aloft.

For all that Schultz stubbornly hid his role for the rest of his life, he managed to find a way into many photographs taken on Suribachi's summit the day the flags were raised.

Schultz was wounded in action on March 13 and left the Marine Corps, with rank of corporal, on October 17, 1945. As a wounded veteran, he was given a leg up in landing a mail-sorting job with the United States Post Office in Los Angeles. He retired in 1981[3] and continued to reside in Los Angeles until his death on May 16, 1995, following a years-long illness.[4]

Proof

A

After Harlon Block was accepted in 1947 as the Marine in Position 1, the line-up of second-flag-raisers became, in Photo A: *Position 1*-Block; *Position 2*-René Gagnon; *Position 3*-John Bradley; *Position 4*-Mike Strank; *Position 5*-Franklin Sousley; *Position 6*-Ira Hayes.

From early 1945 until 2013, Sousley was always said to be in Position 5, but Stephen Foley and Eric Krelle analyzed the equipment the men in positions 3 and 5 carried and, based on other February 23, 1945, photos of Sousley and Bradley, the researchers realized that (a) the equipment on the man in Position 3 matched Sousley's and (b) the equipment on *no* visible flag-raiser matched Bradley's. So, eliminate Bradley as a second-flag-raiser and name Sousley as the man occupying Position 3.

Then who was in Position 5? (Associated Press photo by Joe Rosenthal)

Rifle sling attached to Swivel Stack

Schultz

Sousley

Bill of Soft Cover

Empty Canteen Pouch

B

The Marine at left in Photo B, with the M1 rifle slung on his right shoulder, was thought to be Sousley until Foley and Krelle proved otherwise via an exhaustive equipment check. Look carefully at equipment borne by the Marine at right (in Position 3) and compare it to the detail of Photo C, Joe Rosenthal's second photo, the one of Sousley (and possibly Hayes) holding the raised second flag steady in the wind. You will see an empty canteen cover near Sousley's right hip in Photo B, the flag-raising photo, and, again, at Sousley's right hip in Photo C. Other matching equipment also appears in both photos, such as the bill of Sousley's soft cover poking out from beneath his helmet, ammo pouches, and the camouflage pattern on his helmet cover. In sum, it is sufficient to render the re-identification of Sousley in Position 3 a certainty. (Associated Press photos by Joe Rosenthal)

Empty Canteen Pouch

Bill of Soft Cover

C

The Marine at left in Photo B, with the M1 rifle slung on his right shoulder, was thought to be Sousley until Foley and Krelle proved otherwise via an exhaustive equipment check. Look carefully at equipment borne by the Marine at right (in Position 3) and compare it to the detail of Photo C, Joe Rosenthal's second photo, the one of Sousley (and possibly Hayes) holding the raised second flag steady in the wind. You will see an empty canteen cover near Sousley's right hip in Photo B, the flag-raising photo, and, again, at Sousley's right hip in Photo C. Other matching equipment also appears in both photos, such as the bill of Sousley's soft cover poking out from beneath his helmet, ammo pouches, and the camouflage pattern on his helmet cover. In sum, it is sufficient to render the re-identification of Sousley in Position 3 a certainty. (Associated Press photos by Joe Rosenthal)

D

At least two details in Photo D and Photo E set the Marine at far right apart from all the other Marines who climbed to Suribachi's summit on February 23, 1945: the sling of his M1 rifle is attached at the swivel stack and a small strap hangs down over his left eye. Minute examinations of every available photo taken atop Suribachi on D+4—by a Marine Corps investigative panel in mid-2016—reveals that *each* of these features—helmet-liner strap and rifle sling—are unique to that one Marine. (Official USMC photo by Staff Sergeant Lou Lowery)

During their investigation, one of the Marine panelists broke the code when commenting that, all on its own, it was the unique use of the rifle sling that set that Marine apart from all the other Marines carrying M1 rifles atop Suribachi that day.[5] As far as is known, Foley and Krelle—and everyone who examined their work until mid-2016—completely missed this crucial detail and thus prolonged a simple, quite visible proof that Harold Schultz held Position 3 in the Rosenthal photo. It's as plain as the rifle on his shoulder.

E

See caption for Photo D. (Official USMC Photo by Staff Sergeant Lou Lowery)

F

Sergeant Bill Genaust's movie camera caught the uniquely turned-out Marine—Schultz—as he walked away from the other second-flag-raisers (Photo F) who stayed behind to steady the flagpole. Note in Photo F and Photo G that the upper end of the rifle sling is attached at the swivel stack and a small, faint shadow extends downward from the edge of the helmet to rest over or near the Marine's left eye. (Official USMC photo by Sergeant Bill Genaust)

Sling attached to Swivel Stack

Helmet liner strap over left eye

G

See caption for Photo F. (Official USMC Photo by Staff Sergeant Lou Lowery)

Mystery solved.

CHAPTER 13

The Marines

The ultimate expression of faith in Stephen Foley's and Eric Krelle's work on the second flag-raising—or it was a gigantic leap of faith by some very conservative and normally tight-lipped people—was the embrace garnered from the highest levels of the United States Marine Corps.

On April 19, 2016, following a preliminary assessment of the findings put forth by Stephen Foley and Eric Krelle, General Robert Neller, the commandant of the Marine Corps, announced that he had empaneled a committee of nine senior active duty and retired Marines and civilian experts to investigate the Foley–Krelle claims and produce a definitive finding that would either replace John Bradley as a second-flag-raiser with Harold Schultz or officially sink the claim once and for all. Heading the panel was retired Lieutenant General Jan Huly.

The Huly Panel appointees immediately launched their work at the Marine Corps University in Quantico, Virginia. They studied photos and documents; took in professionally gathered, highly technical forensic evidence; and discussed all types of matters. They wrote their report, which was completed on April 27, and briefed to General Neller for review on May 4. It wasn't until June 23 that the Huly Panel's report, entitled "Second Flag Raising on Iwo Jima," was released to the public. It immediately sent shock waves through the entire tradition-driven Marine Corps extended community world-wide.

In a nutshell, the Huly Panel report raised and enshrined Stephen Foley's and Eric Krelle's work in every one of its aspects to the level of perfection the world expects of a papal directive. Retired Marine Lieutenant Colonel Charles Neimeyer, history PhD, head of the Marine Corps History Division (since retired), and frustrated member of the Huly Panel was moved to bare his feelings in the immediate wake of the finding's release: "Why doesn't [Schultz] say anything to anyone [about his role in raising the second flag]?

That's the mystery." Then, more objectively, "I think he took his secret to the grave." And so he did.

The entire second flag-raising report may be viewed in Appendix B.

The following, written by retired Colonel Mary H. Reinwald, member of the Huly Panel and editor of *Leatherneck* magazine, describes the heart of the report:

The Huly Panel

The Huly panel reviewed the results of the [January 1947] del Valle board [which identified Harlon Block as the right-most flag-raiser, in Position #1 in Chapter 12's Photo A], scrutinizing each individual in the Rosenthal photo, in keeping with the Commandant's direction. The results of the Huly panel, however, differed from the results of the [del Valle] board from 70 years [earlier].

Position #1: Cpl Harlon Block.

No new evidence or recent allegations contradicted Block being the man in Position #1. A comparison of photos taken by Joe Rosenthal throughout the actual flag-raising with the film shot by Sgt Genaust shows the person in Position #1 with equipment and a facial profile consistent with Block. Coupled with Hayes' identification of Block as a flag-raiser in 1946 and confirmation by the del Valle board, no evidence suggests that Block is not the Marine in Position #1.

Position #2: PFC René A. Gagnon.

Similar to Block's identification, no new evidence has called into question [regarding] Gagnon's identification as the second flag-raiser. Upon his return to the States in 1945, Gagnon identified himself as the Marine in Position #2; this identification was later corroborated by both Bradley and Hayes. Although his face is obscured throughout most of the film and photographs, a brief glimpse appears to be Gagnon, and the gear he wore in other clearly identifiable photos is consistent with the gear worn by the Marine in Position #2. As did the del Valle board, the Huly panel continues to believe that Gagnon helped to raise the second flag.

Position #3: PhM2c John Bradley to PFC Franklin Sousley.

In addition to Gagnon's initial identification of Bradley as the individual in Position #3, Bradley himself confirmed this according to a memo to the Director, Division of Public Information, Headquarters, U.S. Marine Corps dated Sept. 24, 1946, ... written for the del Valle board. In his own letter to Gen[eral] del Valle, dated Dec. 26, 1946, Bradley stated, "I was on top of the hill already and when the flag was raised I just jumped up and gave the group a hand." In a letter to the same board dated 16 Dec. 1946, the [Company] E commander, Captain Dave Severance, also agreed that, to the best of his knowledge, Bradley was one of the flag-raisers. The photographic evidence, however, does not support this.

As seen in both the Genaust film and other photographs taken atop Mount Suribachi, the individual in Position #3 is wearing an empty canteen cover, cartridge belt without suspenders, wire cutters, and a soft cover beneath his helmet; he is not carrying a rifle nor wearing a field jacket. Additionally, his trousers are not cuffed.

The Suribachi photographs, including Rosenthal's famous "Gung Ho" photo, also show Bradley without an empty canteen cover, wire cutters, or a soft cover under his helmet. The photos do show Bradley wearing a field jacket with two medical unit 3s, a first aid pack, a K-bar [combat knife], a full canteen cover and suspenders evident. Additionally, his trousers are cuffed, and he is wearing leggings.

[NOTE: Responding to a query from the author—"What was the most compelling evidence for eliminating Bradley as a second-flag-raiser?"—Colonel Reinwald responded: "The gear was to me and most of the board the most important evidence for eliminating Bradley. I'm still very surprised that no one figured it out sooner simply based on what he was and wasn't wearing."][1]

If Bradley is not in Position #3, then who is? Surprisingly, determining the individual in Position #3 was relatively easy after closely analyzing photographs for specific equipment and gear. PFC Sousley, originally identified as the Marine in Position #5, is seen in photographs atop Suribachi wearing an empty canteen cover, a cartridge belt without suspenders, wire cutters, and a soft cover under his helmet. He is not seen wearing a field jacket, and his trousers are not cuffed—his gear is identical to the gear worn by the individual in Position

#3. In addition, there is a moment in the Genaust film and in a Rosenthal photo where the face of the individual is seen briefly. The individual resembles Sousley. In the Huly panel's opinion, Sousley was in Position #3, not Position #5, in Rosenthal's photo.

Position #4: Sgt Michael Strank.

As was the case with Block and Gagnon, no new evidence was discovered to call into question Strank's participation in the second flag-raising. Although the del Valle board determined that the individual in Position #4 was Sgt Strank, the Huly panel worked to confirm this since Position #4 was the most obscured in both the photo and the film. But it was both the film and the Rosenthal photos that once again helped to confirm what was already known.

The Huly panel, after thorough review, ruled out the possibility that the obscured individual in Position #4 could have been Bradley. The individual in Position #4 is not wearing medical unit 3s or any of the other gear that Bradley was. Before the break in the Genaust film, it appears #4 was wearing a soft cover; after the break, however, the individual appears to be wearing a hard cover. The clarity of the film is such that it is not absolute, but one thing is certain based on other photographic evidence—Bradley only wore a helmet. Strank, however, is seen wearing a soft cover beneath his helmet in several photographs.

In addition, in the Genaust film, the ring finger on the left hand of the individual in Position #4 is evident; the finger is bare. Photos clearly identifiable as Strank show that he was not wearing a ring on that finger. Bradley's left hand, however, clearly shows a ring on his ring finger in photos.

Position #5: PFC Franklin Sousley to PFC Harold Schultz.

But if Sousley is in Position #3, who's in Position #5? The equipment, or lack thereof, indicates that it can't be Bradley. Again, Genaust's film and the photos taken by Lowery, Campbell and Rosenthal were thoroughly reviewed and a key piece of evidence helped to greatly simplify the identity—a broken helmet liner strap.

Only one Marine photographed on that fateful day on Mount Suribachi had a broken helmet liner strap hanging from the left side of his helmet, and that was PFC Harold H. Schultz, another member of [Company] E. And, as importantly, the individual in Position #5 had a distinctive rifle. The sling of #5's rifle was attached to the stacking swivel—not to the upper hand guard sling swivel as was appropriate. Again, photos show that the only Marine with his sling attached in that manner was PFC Schultz.

However, and so very puzzling, no previous identification or claim that PFC Schultz was a flag-raiser has ever been found.

Position #6: PFC Hayes.

The easiest of all to identify. In addition to Gagnon and Bradley identifying Hayes from the beginning, Hayes himself admitted that he was a flag-raiser, and the photographic evidence strongly supports these claims.[2]

First Flag

The investigation into the second flag-raising unleashed a torrent of questions and pleas from one branch of the Marine Corps family: wasn't it past time to definitively identify the men who had raised the *first* flag—a job that had never been undertaken at the behest of Marine Corps officialdom. And so the Huly Panel was reconvened under General Neller's aegis at Quantico on July 5, 2016, and worked in secret through to July 8. Following is most of the second Huly Panel report's preliminary statement:

> ... the panel reviewed photographic forensic evidence, photographs, eyewitness statements, and other available evidence related to the first flag raising. To the individuals participating in the Battle of Iwo Jima, the first flag raising was the more significant of the two flag raisings on Mount Suribachi; however, AP photographer Joseph Rosenthal's iconic photograph caused the second flag raising to overshadow the first flag raising event, resulting in less publicity and documentation related to the individuals involved in the first flag raising.
>
> Previous attempts to accurately identify individuals involved in the first flag raising were complicated by the stress of combat, the lack of popular recognition as to the significance of the first flag raising, and the subsequent passage of time. The evidence reviewed by the panel represents an aggregation of years of painstaking research by numerous historians, authors, forensics experts, and others.

The entire first-flag-raising report may be viewed in Appendix A.

It *is* perverse that the second flag has been elevated to the primary position while the first flag—whose raising swelled so many hearts, not least Secretary of the Navy James Forrestal's, and that of the hard-bitten Marine commanding general in the Pacific, Lieutenant General Holland Smith—has been relegated to the secondary role. This perversity can only be laid to the photographic record: the moment of the first flag's raising was not recorded on film, nor were even patriotic words wrought in the triumphal moment, but Joe Rosenthal's superb photo—no matter the ad hoc manner in which it was taken—is truly a one-in-a-trillion symbol that fits comfortably into the role of demonstrating at a glance, and at a deeply emotional level, what Americans have since turned into *the* icon for describing "Americans at war." It is triumphalism at a glance. That photo *still* swells hearts, particularly the hearts of United States Marines, even those Marines born 50 years and more after the end of World War II.

The six official first-flag-raisers anointed by the Huly Panel and the Marine Corps are: First Lieutenant Harold "George" Schrier, the Company E executive officer and patrol leader; Platoon Sergeant Ernest "Boots" Thomas, Jr., leader of Company E's 3rd Platoon; Sergeant Henry "Hank" Hansen, 3rd Platoon right guide; Pharmacist's Mate Second Class John Bradley, the Company E senior corpsman; Corporal Charles "Chuck" Lindberg, flamethrower operator and leader of the 3rd Platoon Assault Squad; and Private Philip Ward, a member of the 3rd Platoon Assault Squad.[3] Platoon Sergeant Thomas was killed in action on March 3, 1945, a week before his 21st birthday;[4] and Sergeant Hansen was killed in action on March 1. All of the others passed away in the normal course of life before the task of determining for all time who was who was ever even considered.[5]

The Question We've All Been Waiting For

Why didn't John Bradley ever just say that he had no part in raising the second flag?—A Speculation

John Bradley has been in the news and on millions of people's minds at least since the 2000 release of his son's—James Bradley's—best-selling book, *Flags of Our Fathers*, and the subsequent release of the Clint Eastwood movie of the same name.

At some point on Iwo Jima, John Bradley probably came down with what was then called war neurosis—what we call post-traumatic stress disorder today, PTSD. By all accounts, he acted as if he was profoundly affected by his taking part in the war—traumatized at least, certainly changed, by the incessant violence and life-threatening danger all around him. Perhaps—thanks in part to the curse of fame derived from the 7th War Bond tour—Bradley never regained his normal self. It is entirely possible that the order this brave and earnest man received from the lieutenant colonel who interviewed him in Washington in April 1945—keep quiet about the official list of second flag-raisers—was taken too much to heart and never rejected by a mind that never grew healthier. He had been threateningly ordered to do nothing to fix history, and that he did: nothing. Only death lifted the burden of balancing between the truth and the profound anxiety of never-ending duty.

If Bradley was indeed suffering from war neurosis, the triggering event might have been the gruesome death of a close buddy, Ralph "Iggy" Ignatowski. Bradley's son James wrote in his book what Doc Bradley told him just once in his life about Ignatowski's death, which John Bradley found difficult to erase from his memory. They were pinned down together on March 4 when a Marine was injured farther along the firing line. Hearing the call for a corpsman, Bradley pulled himself up to answer the call and ran to help out, which included killing an attacking Japanese soldier with his automatic pistol. When Bradley returned to rejoin Ignatowski, the rifleman was nowhere in sight. Bradley had no idea where he had gone, and neither did nearby Marines. Ignatowski had simply disappeared. On March 8, "someone yelled that they'd found [Iggy's] body. They called me over because I was a corpsman. The Japanese had pulled him underground and tortured him. His fingernails ... his tongue ... It was absolutely terrible. I've tried hard to forget all this."[6]

Even in light of the perceived trauma his friend's horrible death administered, Bradley was an authentic hero. He earned a Navy Cross valor medal for saving lives during the attack to surround Suribachi on February 21, 1945. And he was also seriously wounded by mortar shrapnel on March 12, 1945, once again while saving lives at grave risk to his own life. (See Navy Cross citation on page 38.)

The Navy Cross is the nation's second-highest valor medal, right after the Medal of Honor in precedence. It is infrequently but not rarely awarded.

Another clue is the way Bradley lived for the remaining 50 years of his life: morbidly as a small-town undertaker, wounded and reticent to discuss his storied role in the flag-raisings, either of them, for he was an authentic and well-documented (in photos) first-flag-raiser.

Afterword

All of what has transpired with respect to the Iwo Jima flag-raisers over more than seven decades proves what every serious historian has learned the hard way: there is no such thing as settled history, there is still information out there that will confound the orthodoxies of the keepers of history, and almost without a doubt it will be discovered and promulgated by amateur historians who refuse to be bound by such orthodoxies.

Inevitably, I wonder where and when the next changes in the Iwo Jima flags story will emerge.

That said, I fully support the conclusion of one Huly board member, retired Colonel Mary Reinwald, the editor of *Leatherneck* magazine, who concluded her August 2016 article "Examining the Evidence" thusly: "Ironically, the significance of Rosenthal's photo and the Marine Corps War Memorial that it inspired is not who raised the flag, but rather who and what they represented. While the desire to correct the historical record is both understandable and necessary, that moment on top of Mount Suribachi more than 70 years ago will still hold a special place in the hearts of Marines and in the history of the Corps regardless of who raised the flag."[1]

Report of the Huly Board Review of Information Regarding the Identity of the First Flag Raisers Atop Mount Suribachi, Iwo Jima

United States Marine Corps
Marine Corps University
Marine Corps History Division

Report of the Huly Board Review of Information Regarding the Identity of the First Flag Raisers Atop Mount Suribachi, Iwo Jima

Ref:

(a) Nalty, Bernard C. and Danny J. Crawford. *The United States Marines on Iwo Jima: The Battle and the Flag Raisings.* Washington, DC: History and Museums Division, Headquarters, U.S. Marine Corps, 1995.

(b) Alexander, Joseph H. *Closing In: Marines in the Seizure of Iwo Jima.* Washington, DC: History and Museums Division, Headquarters, U.S. Marine Corps, 1994.

(c) Miller, Bill. "The Whine of Snipers' Bullets Comprised the Only Opposition." Vol. 30, no. 9 (September 1947): 10–11.

(d) Marling, Karal Ann and John Wetenhall. *Iwo Jima Monuments, Memories, and the American Hero.* Cambridge, MA: Harvard University Press, 1991.

(e) Albee Jr., Parker Bishop and Keller Cushing Freeman. *Shadow of Suribachi: Raising the Flags on Iwo Jima.* Westport, CT: Praeger Publishers, 1995.

(f) Keene, R.R. "Louis Lowery Captured Leatherneck History on Film." *Leatherneck.* Vol. 79, no. 10 (October 2006): 32–33

(g) Spence, Dustin. "Unraveling the Mysteries of the First Flag Raising." *Leatherneck.* Vol. 79, no. 10 (October 2006): 34–43.

(h) Thomey, Tedd. *Immortal Images: A Personal History of Two Photographers and the Flag Raising on Iwo Jima.* Annapolis: Naval Institute Press, 1996.

(i) Bradley, James with Ron Powers. *Flags of Our Fathers.* New York: Bantam Books, 2000.

(j) Wheeler, Richard. *The Bloody Battle for Suribachi.* New York: Crowell, 1965.

(k) Conner, Howard M. *The Spearhead: The World War II History of the 5th Marine Division.* Washington, DC: Infantry Journal Press, 1950.

(l) Wells, John Keith. *Iwo Jima: "Give Me Fifty Men Not Afraid to Die."* Quality Publications, 1995.

Encl:

(1) CMC letter dated 05 July 2016, Precept Convening the Huly Board to Review Information Regarding the Identity of the First Flag Raisers atop Mount Suribachi, Iwo Jima [Cover Letter Ref (a)]

(2) Reference Photographs of the First Flag Raising on Iwo Jima, 23 February 1945 with Annotations Determined by History Division on 01 July 2016.

(3) Excerpts from "Report of the Huly Board Review of New Information Regarding the Identity of the Second Flag Raisers atop Mount Suribachi, Iwo Jima."

(4) Personnel Determined by History Division on 23 June 2003 to have been Members of the Patrol that Occupied Mount Suribachi on 23 February 1945

(5) Annotated "Gung Ho" Photograph taken by Joe Rosenthal of the Associated Press, 23 February 1945. Defense Media Activity. Accessed 05 July 2016, http://www.5thmarinedivision.com/uploads/8/1/0/6/8106876/8416758_orig.jpg.

(6) Excerpts, Muster Roll of 2d Battalion, 28th Marines (April 1944; October 1944; January 1945; February 1945)

(7) Excerpts, Muster Roll of Headquarters Battalion, 5th Marine Division (January 1945)

(8) Evaluation of Casualty Cards for Company E, 2d Battalion, 28th Marines, 5th Division, determined by History Division on 01 July 2016; Casualty Cards for Company E, 2d Battalion, 28th Marines, 5th Division, based on February 1945 Muster Roll

(9) Eyewitness account by PFC Raymond Jacobs

(10) Excerpts, Muster Roll of 3d Battalion, 27th Marines (February 1945)
(11) Excerpts, Muster Roll of 2d Battalion, 27th Marines (February 1945)

Authority
The Board was convened by CMC Precept letter dated 05 July 2016. [Encl (1)]

Board Composition

President	LtGen Jan C. Huly, USMC (Ret)
Member	BGen Jason Q. Bohm, USMC, CG, TCOM
Member	Colonel Keil R. Gentry, USMC (Ret)
Member	Colonel Mary H. Reinwald, USMC (Ret), Editor, *Leatherneck*
Member	Sergeant Major Gary Smith, USMC, SgtMaj, SYSCOM
Member	Sergeant Major David L. Maddux, USMC, SgtMaj, EDCOM
Member	Sergeant Major Richard A. Hawkins, USMC (Ret)
Member	Dr. Sarandis Papadopoulos, Navy Department Secretariat
Historian Member/Recorder	Dr. Charles P. Neimeyer, Director, History Division
Administrative Support	Dr. Breanne Robertson

Date and Location
The Huly Board convened at the Gray Research Center, Quantico, VA, at 0900 on 05 July 2016. The Board concluded at 1600 on 08 July 2016.

Preliminary Statement
At the direction of the Commandant of the Marine Corps the Huly Board that analyzed the second flag raising on Mount Suribachi, Iwo Jima, 23 February 1945 reconvened in order to review the photographic evidence and claims related to the identity of the participants in the first flag raising.

In accordance with Enclosure (1), the panel reviewed photographic forensic evidence, photographs, eyewitness statements, and other available evidence related to the first flag raising. To the individuals participating in the Battle of Iwo Jima, the first flag raising was the more significant of the two flag raisings on Mount Suribachi; however, AP photographer Joseph Rosenthal's iconic photograph caused the second flag raising to overshadow the first flag raising event, resulting in less publicity and documentation related to the individuals involved in the first flag raising.

Previous attempts to accurately identify individuals involved in the first flag raising were complicated by the stress of combat, the lack of popular recognition as to the significance of the first flag raising, and the subsequent passage of time. The evidence reviewed by the panel represents an aggregation of years of painstaking research by numerous historians, authors, forensics experts, and others.

Findings of Fact

1. Current official Marine Corps records identify the first flag raisers as:

   a. 1stLt Harold G. Schrier [Ref (a), (b)]
   b. PltSgt Ernest I. Thomas, Jr. [Ref (a), (b)]
   c. Sgt Henry O. Hansen [Ref (a), (b)]
   d. Cpl Charles W. Lindberg [Ref (a), (b)]
   e. PFC Louis C. Charlo [Ref (a), (b)]
   f. PFC James R. Michels [Ref (a), (b)]

2. Early on the morning of 23 February 1945 LtCol Chandler W. Johnson, CO, 2/28, ordered a team to ascend Mount Suribachi to conduct route reconnaissance and determine enemy disposition on the summit. [Ref (c), p. 11]

3. The individuals who comprised the reconnaissance team on Mount Suribachi were Sgt Sherman B. Watson, Cpl George Mercer, PFC Theodore White, and PFC Louis C. Charlo, all members of F/2/28. [Ref (c), (e) and Encl (2), p. 2]

4. The reconnaissance team encountered no enemy activity on the summit of Mount Suribachi. [Ref (e), p. 41]

5. On 23 February 1945, CO 2/28, LtCol Johnson, ordered XO, E/2/28, 1stLt Harold G. Schrier, to lead a platoon-sized patrol with the mission to secure the top of Mount Suribachi and raise the American flag. [Ref (a)–(b), (d), (j)]

6. At the base of Mount Suribachi 1stLt G. Greeley Wells, battalion adjutant for 2/28, provided an American flag to 1stLt Schrier on orders from the battalion commander prior to the patrol's ascent. [Ref (a), (c), (j)]

7. The patrol led by 1stLt Schrier consisted of 3d Platoon, E/2/28, reinforced by other elements of 2/28, and Staff Sergeant Louis R. Lowery,

a *Leatherneck* photographer assigned to the 5th Marine Division. [Ref (a)–(b), (f)–(g) and Encl (6)–(8)]

8. 1stLt Schrier's patrol departed the base of Mount Suribachi at approximately 0830 and passed the reconnaissance team descending from the summit. [Ref (b), (d), (f) and Encl (2), p. 3]

9. The reconnaissance team returned to F/2/28 at the base of Mount Suribachi shortly after they passed the Schrier patrol proceeding up the mountain. [Ref (d), p. 41]

10. The following individuals have been identified as members of the patrol led by 1stLt Schrier that occupied the summit of Mount Suribachi at approximately 1000:

    a. 1stLt Harold G. Schrier [Ref (a), (d), (f), (g), (j), (l)]

    b. PltSgt Ernest I. Thomas, Jr. [Ref (a), (d), (f), (g) and Encl (6), (8)]

    c. SSgt Louis R. Lowery [Ref (a), (d), (f), (g)]

    d. Sgt Henry O. Hansen [Ref (a), (d), (g) and Encl (6), (8)]

    e. Sgt Kenneth D. Midkiff [Ref (d), (j) and Encl (6), (8)]

    f. Sgt Howard M. Snyder [Ref (d), (g), (l) and Encl (6), (8)]

    g. PhM2c John H. Bradley [Ref (d), (g) and Encl (6)]

    h. Cpl Raymond E. Jacobs [Ref (g), (l) and Encl (6)]

    i. Cpl Harold P. Keller [Ref (c)-(d), (j), (l) and Encl (6)]

    j. Cpl Robert A. Leader [Ref (d), (f), (j), (l) and Encl (6), (8)]

    k. Cpl Charles W. Lindberg [Ref (a); (d); (f)–(g); (j); (l) and Encl (6), (8)]

    l. PFC Graydon W. Dyce [Ref (j), p. 140, 143 and Encl (6)]

    m. PFC Clarence H. Garrett [Ref (c)–(d), (j), (l) and Encl (6)]

    n. PFC Thomas J. Hermanek, Jr. [Ref (l), p. 241 and Encl (6)]

    o. PFC Donald S. Howell [Ref (i), p. 203 and Encl (6)]

    p. PFC Raymond H. Larsen [Encl (5), (6)]

    q. PFC James R. Michels [Ref (a), (c)–(d), (f)–(h), (j) and Encl (6), (8)]

    r. PFC Orval E. Mosley [Ref (l), p. 241 and Encl (10)]

    s. PFC Manuel Panizo [Ref (d), (j), (l) and Encl (6), (8)]

    t. PFC James A. Robeson [Ref (c)–(d), (f); (j), (l) and Encl (6), (8)]

    u. PFC Leo J. Rozek [Ref (d), (f), (j), (l) and Encl (6)]

    v. PFC John T. Schmitt [Ref (l), p. 241 and Encl (6), (8)]

    w. PFC Harold H. Schultz [Ref (g), p. 37 and Encl (6)]

    x. PFC Fred J. Walcsak [Encl (5), (6)]

    y. Pvt Kenneth S. Espenes [Ref (j), p. 143 and Encl (6)]

z. Pvt Robert D. Goode [Ref (d), (l) and Encl (6), (8)]

aa. Pvt Philip L. Ward [Ref (d), (g), (i) and Encl (6)]

11. The following individuals were assigned to 3d Platoon, E/2/28, as of 23 February 1945 but cannot be confirmed as being members of the Schrier patrol:

   a. Cpl James E. Hagstrom [Ref (j), p. 143 and Encl (6), (8)]
   b. PFC Clarence R. Hipp [Ref (j), p. 143 and Encl (6), (8)]
   c. PFC William J. McNulty [Ref (j), p. 143 and Encl (6), (8)]
   d. Pvt Clark L. Gaylord [Ref (j), p. 143 and Encl (6), (8)]
   e. Pvt James D. Breitenstein [Ref (j), p. 143 and Encl (6), (8)]
   f. Pvt Charles E. Schott [Ref (j), p. 143 and Encl (6), (8)]

12. All of the members in the patrol led by 1stLt Schrier cannot be identified due to insufficient evidence. [Ref (a)–(l) and Encl (6)–(8)]

13. When the patrol reached the top of the mountain, its members dispersed along the crest of the crater to occupy security positions while the headquarters element looked for a suitable place to raise the flag. [Ref (d), (j)]

14. Cpl Robert A. Leader and PFC Leo J. Rozek found the pipe to which the first flag was affixed. [Ref (d)–(f); (j), (l)]

15. SSgt Lowery photographed the preparation of the first flag. [Ref (d), (e), (f), (l) and Encl (2), pp. 4–8]

16. The following individuals affixed the first flag to the pipe:

   a. 1stLt Harold G. Schrier [Ref (d)–(f); (j) and Encl (2), pp. 4–7]
   b. PltSgt Ernest I. Thomas, Jr. [Ref (d)–(f); (j) and Encl (2), pp. 4–7]
   c. Sgt Henry O. Hansen [Ref (d)–(e); (j) and Encl (2), pp. 4–7]
   d. Cpl Charles W. Lindberg [Ref (d)–(e); (j) and Encl (2), pp. 4–7]
   e. Pvt Philip L. Ward [Ref (g), p. 35 and Encl (2), pp. 4, 7]

17. The flagpole was carried horizontally for a short distance from the place where it was prepared to the location where it was raised. [Ref (e), p. 39]

18. The following individuals were either touching or within reach of the flagpole just prior to the first flag being raised:

   a. 1stLt Harold G. Schrier [Encl (2), p. 8]
   b. PltSgt Ernest I. Thomas, Jr. [Encl (2), p. 8]

    c. Sgt Henry O. Hansen [Encl (2), p. 8]
    d. PhM2c John H. Bradley [Encl (2), p. 8]
    e. Cpl Charles W. Lindberg [Encl (2), p. 8]
    f. Pvt Philip L. Ward [Encl (2), p. 8]

19. The first flag was raised on the summit of Mount Suribachi at approximately 1030. [Ref (a–l)]
20. SSgt Lowery was reloading the film in his camera as the first flag was being raised. [Ref (d), (e)]
21. No photographs or film are known to exist that depict the actual raising of the first flag. [Ref (a)–(l) and Encl (2)]
22. SSgt Lowery resumed taking photographs of the first flag immediately after it was raised. [Ref (d)–(f), (g) and Encl (2), pp. 9–15]
23. The following individuals were in contact with the flagpole on the summit of Mount Suribachi immediately after the first flag was raised:

    a. PltSgt Ernest I. Thomas, Jr. [Encl (2), pp. 9–10, 15]
    b. Sgt Henry O. Hansen [Encl (2), pp. 9–13, 15]
    c. PhM2c John H. Bradley [Ref (g) and Encl (2), pp. 9–15]
    d. Pvt Philip L. Ward [Ref (g) and [Encl (2), pp. 9–15]

24. Immediately after the event, LtCol Johnson and 1stLt Schrier communicated via radio regarding the first flag raising. [Encl (2), pp. 11, 13–15 and Encl (9)]
25. The following individuals provided support in the immediate vicinity of the first flag raising:

    a. Sgt Howard M. Snyder, Security [Ref (g), (j) and Encl (2), pp. 9–10, 13–15]
    b. Cpl Raymond E. Jacobs, Radio Operator [Ref (g), (l) and Encl (2), pp. 9–15]
    c. PFC James R. Michels, Security [Ref (g)–(h), (j) and Encl (2), pp. 12]
    d. PFC Harold H. Schultz, Security [Ref (g), p. 37 and Encl (2), pp. 9–14]
    e. PFC James A. Robeson, Security [Ref (c), (f); (l)]

26. Of the photographic evidence available to and reviewed by this panel, none show PFC Charlo in the vicinity of the first flag as it was being raised. [Encl (2)]

27. A patrol led by Capt Arthur H. Naylor, Jr., CO, F/2/28, and consisting of members of F/2/28 ascended the summit to reinforce security after the first flag raising and prior to the second flag raising at approximately 1300. [Ref (e), p. 46]
28. All of the members in the patrol led by Capt Naylor cannot be identified due to insufficient evidence. [Ref (a)–(l)]
29. LT Charles F. Suver, CHC, USNR, and his assistant, Sgt James E. Fisk, ascended the mountain after the first flag raising and prior to the second flag raising. [Ref (d), pp. 42, 53 and Encl (2)]
30. In addition to the above, the following individuals were present on the summit after the first flag raising and prior to the "Gung Ho" photograph taken immediately after the second flag raising by AP photographer Joseph Rosenthal:

    a. Sgt William H. Genaust [Encl (2), p. 16; (3), (7)]
    b. Sgt Michael Strank [Encl (3), (5)]
    c. Sgt Sherman B. Watson [Ref (d), p. 41]
    d. Cpl Harlon H. Block [Encl (3)]
    e. PFC Louis R. Burmeister [Ref (e), pp. 62–66 and Encl (2), p. 18]
    f. PFC George Burns [Ref (e), pp. 62–66 and Encl (2), p. 16]
    g. PFC Louis C. Charlo [Ref (d), p. 41 and Encl (2), p. 18]
    h. PFC Rene A. Gagnon [Encl (3)]
    i. PFC Ira H. Hayes [Encl (3), (5)]
    j. PFC Franklin R. Sousley [Encl (3), (5)]
    k. PFC John R. Thurman [Encl (5), (11)]
    l. PFC Theodore White [Ref (d), p. 41]
    m. Pvt Robert W. Campbell [Encl (2), p. 16; (3), (7)]
    n. Civ Joseph J. Rosenthal [Encl (2), p. 16; (3)]

Opinions

1. The following six individuals raised the first flag:

    a. 1stLt Harold G. Shrier [FF 1, 5, 6–8, 10, 12, 15–19, 22]
    b. PltSgt Ernest I. Thomas, Jr. [FF 1, 7–8, 10, 15–19. 22–23]
    c. Sgt Henry O. Hansen [FF 1, 7–8. 10, 15–19, 22–23]
    d. PhM2c John H. Bradley [FF 7–8, 10, 17–19, 22–23]
    e. Cpl Charles W. Lindberg [FF 1, 7–8, 10, 15–19, 22]
    f. Pvt Philip L. Ward [FF 7–8, 10, 15–19, 22–23]

2. The following individuals did not raise the first flag as previously indicated in the official historical record of the Marine Corps:

   a. PFC Louis C. Charlo [FF 1–3, 8–9, 13, 20–22, 26]
   b. PFC James R. Michels [FF 1, 7–8, 10, 13, 20–22, 25]

3. Although PFC Charlo did not raise the first flag, he was a member of the reconnaissance team prior to the first flag raising and later returned to the summit as security reinforcement prior to the raising of the second flag. [FF 2–4, 8–9, 13, 20–22, 26]
4. Although PFC Michels did not raise the first flag, he provided security in the immediate vicinity of the event. [FF 5, 7–8, 10, 13, 20–22, 25]
5. PFC Michels was previously identified as a participant in the first flag raising due to his prominent positioning in the photograph taken by SSgt Lowery immediately after the event. [FF 1, 13, 20–22, 25]
6. There may be additional members of the patrol led by 1stLt Schrier, but they cannot be identified due to insufficient evidence. [FF 5, 7–8, 10–12, 30]
7. There may be additional members of the patrol led by Capt Naylor, but they cannot be identified due to insufficient evidence. [FF 27–28, 30]
8. Additional individuals may have been present on the summit during the flag raising events on 23 February 1945, but they cannot be identified due to insufficient evidence. [FF 1–30]

Recommendations

1. That the records of Headquarters U.S. Marine Corps reflect the identification of the individuals in the first flag raising as follows:

   a. 1stLt Harold G. Schrier
   b. PltSgt Ernest I. Thomas, Jr.
   c. Sgt Henry O. Hansen
   d. PhM2c John H. Bradley
   e. Cpl Charles W. Lindberg
   f. Pvt Philip L. Ward

2. That the Commandant of the Marine Corps should inform the Secretary of the Navy, Chief of Naval Operations and Medical Officer of the Marine Corps of the results of this panel before they are made public.

3. That the Commandant of the Marine Corps should inform the appropriate relatives of 1stLt Harold G. Schrier, PltSgt Ernest I. Thomas, Jr., Sgt Henry O. Hansen, Cpl Charles W. Lindberg, PFC Louis C. Charlo, PFC James R. Michels, Pvt Philip L. Ward and PhM2c John H. Bradley of the results of this panel before they are made public.

4. That the Commandant of the Marine Corps should issue a public statement regarding the correct identification of the first flag raisers. This statement should include acknowledgement of the collective efforts of all who contributed to telling the story of the sacrifices and heroic achievements of all Marines, Sailors and Coast Guardsmen during the battle of Iwo Jima.

5. That the Commandant of the Marine Corps recognize that all previous efforts at identification were conducted in good faith and that no official blame be assessed for previous inaccuracies in the historical record.

6. That the Commandant of the Marine Corps direct that this panel report and associated records be deposited in the Marine Corps History Division's archives.

7. That the Office of Legislative Affairs should inform appropriate Members of Congress and congressional staff of the results of this panel before they are made public.

8. That Headquarters U.S. Marine Corps should make public the findings of this panel.

9. That the Commandant of the Marine Corps should coordinate the public release of the findings of this panel with the Office of U.S. Marine Corps Communication.

Report of the Huly Board Review of New Information Regarding the Identity of the Second Flag Raisers Atop Mount Suribachi, Iwo Jima

United States Marine Corps
Marine Corps University
Marine Corps History Division

Report of the Huly Board Review of New Information Regarding the Identity of the Second Flag Raisers Atop Mount Suribachi, Iwo Jima

Ref:
(a) Wells, John Keith. *"Give Me Fifty Marines Not Afraid to Die": Iwo Jima*. Washington, DC: Quality Publications, 1995.

(b) Nalty, Bernard C. and Danny J. Crawford. *The United States Marines on Iwo Jima: The Battle and the Flag Raisings*. Washington, DC: History and Museums Division, Headquarters, U.S. Marine Corps, 1995.

(c) Spence, Dustin. "Unraveling the Mysteries of the First Flag Raising." *Leatherneck*. LXXIX, No. 10 (October 2006): 34–43

(d) Marling, Karal Ann and John Wetenhall. *Iwo Jima Monuments, Memories, and the American Hero*. Cambridge, MA: Harvard University Press, 1991.

(e) Keene, R.R. "Louis Lowery Captured Leatherneck History on Film." *Leatherneck*. LXXIX, No. 10 (October 2006): 32.

(f) Albee Jr., Parker Bishop and Keller Cushing Freeman. *Shadow of Suribachi: Raising the Flags on Iwo Jima*. Westport, CT: Praeger Publishers, 1995.

(g) Rosenthal, Joe. "Gung Ho" Photograph, 23 February 1945. Defense Media Activity. Accessed 21 April 2016, http://media.dma.mil/1945/Feb/23/176790/-1/-1/0/450223- M-0000W-007.jpg.

(h) Bradley, James with Ron Powers. *Flags of Our Fathers.* New York, NY: Bantam Books, 2000.

(i) Buell, Hal, ed. *Uncommon Valor, Common Virtue.* New York, NY: Penguin, 2006.

Encl:

(1) CMC letter dated 19 April 2016, Precept Convening the Huly Board to Review New Information Regarding the Identity of the Second Flag Raisers atop Mount Suribachi, Iwo Jima [Ref (a)]

(2) Report of the Board Appointed to Determine the Identity of Personnel Who Participated in the Mt. Suribachi Flag Raising as Photographed by Mr. Joe Rosenthal of the Associated Press [De Valle Board Report]

(3) Excerpts, Muster Roll of 2d Battalion, 28th Marines (April 1944; October 1944; January 1945; February 1945); Casualty Card of PFC Schultz

(4) Excerpts, Muster Roll of Headquarters Battalion, 5th Marine Division

(5) Casualty Card of Sgt Genaust

(6) Genaust, "Iwo Jima D+4," Roll 13

(7) Casualty Card of Cpl Block

(8) Casualty Card of Sgt Strank

(9) Casualty Card of PFC Sousley

(10) Hansen, Matthew. "New Mystery Arises from Iconic Iwo Jima Image." *Omaha World-Herald.* 23 November 2014. Accessed 21 April 2016, http://dataomaha.com/media/news/2014/iwo-jima/.

(11) Plaxton, Michael. "Analysis of Digital Images for Lucky 8 TV." Forensic Video Consulting, 17 December 2015.

Authority

The Board was convened by CMC Precept letter dated 19 April 2016. [Encl (1)]

Board Composition

President	LtGen Jan C. Huly, USMC (Ret)
Member	Colonel Keil R. Gentry, USMC, Director, MCWAR

Member	Colonel Jason Q. Bohm, USMC, Director, EWS
Member	Colonel Mary H. Reinwald, USMC (Ret), Editor, *Leatherneck*
Member	Sergeant Major Justin D. LeHew, USMC, SgtMaj, TECOM
Member	Sergeant Major David L. Maddux, USMC, SgtMaj, EDCOM
Member	Sergeant Major Richard A. Hawkins, USMC (Ret)
Member	Dr. Sarandis Papadopoulos, Navy Department Secretariat
Historian Member/Recorder	Dr. Charles P. Neimeyer, Director, History Division
Administrative Support	Dr. Breanne Robertson

Date and Location

The Huly Board convened at the Gray Research Center, Quantico, VA, at 0900 on 19 April 2016. The Board concluded at 1600 on 27 April 2016.

Preliminary Statement

In accordance with enclosure (1), the Huly Board reviewed enhanced photographic forensic evidence, photographs, film, eyewitness statements, and other available evidence related to the flag raising. The evidence reviewed by the Board represents an aggregation of years of painstaking research by numerous historians, authors, forensics experts, and others.

On 23 February 1945, as part of the operation to take Iwo Jima, 2d Battalion, 28th Marine Regiment (2/28) was assigned the mission of securing Mount Suribachi. As planned once the Marines secured the summit, they raised the American flag. As that first flag snapped in the wind, cheers rose from the beach, ships sounded their horns, and Secretary of the Navy Forrestal turned to MajGen H.M. Smith and said, "Holland, this means a Marine Corps for another 500 years." At the time, the first flag raising was the more significant of the two flag raisings to those present. The second flag raising would likely have been lost to history, if it were not for Mr. Joseph "Joe" J. Rosenthal's iconic photograph. Given this context, the stress of combat, and the passage of time, it is not surprising that facts surrounding the second flag raising have been difficult to determine.

The 1947 del Valle Board focused primarily on correcting the identification of the individual in Position #1. That Board determined the identities of the six flag raisers in Mr. Rosenthal's photograph of the second flag raising atop Mount Suribachi as shown in Figure 1. The del Valle Board relied on witness statements and the iconic photograph to identify the flag raisers. Since 1947, additional evidence has come to light and there have been significant advances in photographic forensics.

Identifying personnel in specific locations and times based upon the positioning of visible combat gear and clothing is difficult. People may reposition their gear and clothing, thereby changing their appearance in photographs and film. Nevertheless, physical recognition of faces, body positions, and combat gear present the strongest corroborative evidence this Board had to consider at this time.

Figure 1: The del Valle Board Determination of the Identities of the Six Flag Raisers in Mr. Rosenthal's Photograph

The Huly Board used the position numbers indicated in Figure 2 below to reference individual locations.

Figure 2: Huly Board Position Reference

Findings of Fact

1. On 23 February 1945, Sgt Michael Strank (275228), Cpl Harlon H. Block (820595), PFC Ira H. Hayes (448804), and PFC Franklin R. Sousley (942297) were members of the same squad in E/2/28. [Encl (2)]
2. On 23 February 1945, PFC Harold H. Schultz (555867) was a mortarman with E/2/28. [Encl (3)]
3. On 23 February 1945, PhM2c John H. Bradley (8681681) was a corpsman with HQ/2/28. [Encl (3)]
4. On 23 February 1945, PFC Rene A. Gagnon (808267) was the Battalion Commander's Runner from E/2/28. [Ref (b), p. 8]
5. On 23 February 1945, SSgt Louis R. Lowery was a *Leatherneck* photographer assigned as a combat cameraman to 5th Marine Division. [Encl (4)]
6. On 23 February 1945, Sgt William H. Genaust was assigned as a combat cameraman to 5th Marine Division. [Encl (4), Encl (5)]
7. On 23 February 1945, PFC Robert R. Campbell was assigned as a combat cameraman to 5th Marine Division. [Encl (4)]
8. On 23 February 1945, CO 2/28, LtCol Chandler W. Johnson, ordered XO, E/2/28, 1stLt Harold G. Schrier, to lead a platoon-sized patrol with the mission to secure the top of Mount Suribachi and raise the American flag. [Ref (b), p. 5]
9. SSgt Lowery and PhM2c Bradley were members of the patrol. [Ref (d), p. 44]
10. The first flag was raised at approximately 1020 on 23 February 1945 atop Mount Suribachi. [Ref (b), p. 5)]
11. SSgt Lowery took photographs of members in the vicinity before and after the first flag raising. [Ref (c), p. 34-43)]
12. PhM2c Bradley participated in the raising of the first flag atop Mount Suribachi. [(Ref (c), p. 34-43)]
13. PFC Schultz was in the immediate vicinity of the first flag raising atop Mount Suribachi. [Ref (c), p. 34-43)]
14. On 23 February 1945, CO 2/28, LtCol Johnson, ordered a resupply patrol to carry a second, larger flag to replace the first flag. [Ref (b), p. 8]
15. On 23 February 1945, Mr. Rosenthal was a photographer with the Associated Press (AP). [Encl (2)]
16. On 23 February 1945, Sgt Strank, Cpl Block, PFC Hayes, PFC Sousley, and PFC Gagnon were members of the resupply patrol, accompanied

by Mr. Rosenthal, Sgt Genaust, and PFC Campbell, that carried the second flag to the top of Mount Suribachi. [Ref (d) and Encl (2)]

17. The second flag was raised at approximately 1220 on 23 February 1945 as the first flag was simultaneously lowered. [Ref (e), p. 32]

18. Sgt Genaust filmed the preparation and raising of the second flag. [Encl (6)]

19. Sgt Genaust stopped filming the preparation of the second flag prior to it being raised, and he moved to a new position. [Ref (d), p. 67 and Encl (6)]

20. Before the break in filming, the Genaust film shows four individuals focused on getting into position on the flag pole. [Encl (6)]

21. Sgt Genaust resumed filming after an undetermined period of time. [Encl (6)]

22. After the break in filming and just prior to the raising of the flag, the Genaust film shows that the second flag raisers were focused in the direction of the first flag and not on each other. [Encl (6)]

23. Sgt Genaust continued filming and captured six individuals raising the second flag. [Encl (6)]

24. Mr. Rosenthal photographed the second flag being raised. [Encl (2)]

25. PFC Campbell photographed the first flag being lowered while the second flag was being raised (see Figure 3). [Ref (f)]

26. Shortly after the second flag was raised, Mr. Rosenthal took a group photo around the second flag, which became known as the "Gung Ho" photograph (see Figure 4). [Ref (f)]

27. Cpl Block was killed in action (KIA) on Iwo Jima on 1 March 1945. [Encl (7)]

28. Sgt Strank was KIA on Iwo Jima on 1 March 1945. [Encl (8)]

29. PhM2c Bradley was wounded on 12 March 1945 and evacuated by air on 13 March 1945. [Ref (b), p. 11]

30. PFC Sousley was KIA on Iwo Jima on or about 21 March 1945. [Encl (9)]

31. PFC Gagnon made the original identifications of the second flag raisers in Mr. Rosenthal's iconic photograph upon his return to the United States. [Encl (2)]

32. PhM2c Bradley, Sgt Strank, PFC Sousley, PFC Hayes, and PFC Schultz are identified in Mr. Rosenthal's "Gung Ho" photograph (see Figure 4). [Ref (g), Ref (h), and Ref (f)]

Figure 3: Cropped Photograph of the First Flag being Lowered and the Second Flag Being Raised taken by PFC Campbell

Figure 4: Annotated "Gung Ho" Photograph taken by Mr. Rosenthal

33. At some later time, PFC Schultz identified himself as the fifth individual from the right in an inscription on the "Gung Ho" photograph. [Encl (10)]

34. The 1947 del Valle Board determined the individual in Position #1 is Cpl Harlon Block. [Encl (2)]

35. No known evidence contradicts the findings of the del Valle Board as to the identification of the individual in Position #1. [Ref (a)–(h) and Encl (1)–(11)]

36. The individual in Position #1 is wearing a strap across his back that is consistent with a bandoleer (see Figure 1). [Encl (2)]

37. The Genaust film shows all 6 flag raisers positioned around the upright pole. [Encl (6)]

38. Sgt Genaust stopped filming for a second time. [Encl (6)]

39. Sgt Genaust resumed filming after an indeterminate number of seconds. The gear worn on the individuals holding the flag pole is consistent with the persons from Positions #1, #3, #4, and #6 shown before the second break in filming. [Encl (6)]

40. During the break, Mr. Rosenthal moved slightly to the right of his original position. In this way he was able to capture a profile view of the individual in Position #1, a frontal view of the individual in Position #3, and a partial view of the individual in Position #6 (see Figure 5). [Ref (i)]

41. Sgt Genaust continued filming and captured the individuals in Positions #1, #3, #4, and #6 are shown stabilizing the flag pole, while the individual in Position #5 is walking away from the flag. [Encl (6)]

42. Mr. Rosenthal took a contemporaneous photograph of the individual from Position #1 shown in the Genaust film where his face and equipment are clearly seen (see Figure 5). [Ref (i)]

43. The face of the individual in Position #1 in the contemporaneous photograph by Mr. Rosenthal resembles the service photograph of Cpl Harlon Block (see Figure 5). [Ref (i)]

44. The 1947 del Valle Board determined the individual in Position #2 is PFC Gagnon. [Encl (2)]

45. PFC Gagnon identified himself as the individual in Position #2. [Encl (2)]

46. The Genaust film and PFC Campbell's photograph of the two flags show the individual in Position #2 with a rifle slung over his shoulder, which is consistent with PFC Gagnon's T/O weapon. [Encl (6)]

47. The momentary glimpse of the face in Position #2 appears to be PFC Gagnon. [Encl (6)]

48. The 1947 del Valle Board determined the individual in Position #3 is PhM2c Bradley. [Encl (2)]

49. PhM2c Bradley identified himself as the individual in Position #3. [Encl (2)]

50. The individual in Position #3 is wearing an empty canteen cover, cartridge belt without suspenders, wire cutters, soft cover under helmet, and is not carrying a rifle nor wearing a field jacket. Additionally, his trousers are not cuffed. [Encl (11)]

51. Photographs show PFC Sousley wearing an empty canteen cover, cartridge belt without suspenders, wire cutters, soft cover under helmet, and he is not wearing a field jacket. Additionally, PFC Sousley's trousers are not cuffed. [Encl (11)]

52. Photographs show PhM2c Bradley not wearing an empty canteen cover, wire cutters, or a soft cover under his helmet. He is shown wearing a field jacket, two medical unit 3s, first aid pack, K-bar, full

Figure 5: Cropped and Annotated Photo of Individuals Securing the Second Flag taken by Mr. Rosenthal

canteen cover, and suspenders. Additionally, his trousers are cuffed, and he is wearing leggings. [Encl (11)]

53. The Genaust film shows the individual in Position #3 moving into a subsequent position where his face and his equipment are clearly seen. [Encl (6)]

54. Mr. Rosenthal took a contemporaneous photograph of the individual from Position #3 shown in the Genaust film where his face and equipment are clearly seen (see Figure 5). [Encl (11)]

55. Photographic analysis of Mr. Rosenthal's photograph identifies the individual from Position#3 as PFC Sousley. [Encl (11)]

56. The 1947 del Valle Board determined the individual in Position #4 is Sgt Strank. [Encl (2)]

57. The Genaust film shows the individual in Position #4 moving into a subsequent position where a portion of his left hand is visible. [Encl (6)]

58. Mr. Rosenthal took a contemporaneous photograph of the individual, who is shown in the Genaust film in Position #4, where the bare ring finger of his left hand is clearly visible. [Encl (11)]

59. A ring is clearly visible on the ring finger of the left hand of PhM2c Bradley in photographs PFC Campbell (see Figure 6) and SSgt Lowery shot prior to the second flag raising. [Encl (11)]

60. No ring is visible on the ring finger of the left hand of Sgt Strank in the "Gung Ho" photograph. [Ref (g)]

61. No medical unit 3s, or other gear worn on the torso, are visible on the individual in Position#4. [Encl (6) and (10)]

62. Sgt Strank is not wearing any gear other than a helmet over a soft cover in the "Gung Ho" photograph. [Ref (g)]

63. In the Genaust film before the break, the individual in Position #4 appears to be wearing a soft cover. [Encl (6)]

64. In the Genaust film after the break, the individual in Position #4 appears to be wearing a helmet. [Encl (6)]

65. Of the photographs available to and reviewed by this Board, none show PhM2c Bradley wearing a soft cover on Mount Suribachi. [Ref (a)–(h) and Encl (1)–(11)]

66. Sgt Strank was wearing a soft cover under his helmet in the "Gung Ho" photograph. [Ref (g)]

67. The 1947 del Valle Board determined the individual in Position #5 is PFC Sousley. [Encl (2)]

68. The individual in Position #5 has a broken helmet liner strap hanging from the left side of his helmet. [Encl (11)]
69. PFC Schultz has been identified in photographs as having a broken helmet liner strap hanging from the left side of his helmet. [Encl (11)]
70. From the photographs and film footage examined, no one else has been identified atop Mount Suribachi with a broken helmet liner strap hanging from the left side of his helmet. [Ref (a)–(h) and Encl (1)–(11)]
71. The individual in Position #5 has a sling attached to the stacking swivel instead of being properly attached to the upper hand guard sling swivel of his rifle. [Encl (11)]
72. PFC Schultz has been identified in photographs as having a sling attached to the stacking swivel of his rifle. [Encl (11)]
73. From the photographs and film footage examined, no one else has been identified atop Mount Suribachi carrying a rifle with a sling attached to the stacking swivel of his rifle. [Ref (a)–(h) and Encl (1)–(11)]
74. The individual in Position #5 has a bulging right front field jacket pocket. [Encl (11)]
75. PFC Schultz has been identified in photographs as having a bulging right front field jacket pocket. [Encl (11)]
76. There is no indication PFC Schultz or anyone else ever mentioned him as raising the flag on Iwo Jima. [Encl (10)]
77. The 1947 del Valle Board determined the individual in Position #6 is PFC Hayes. [Encl (2)]
78. PFC Hayes identified himself as the individual in Position #6. [Encl (2)]
79. The Genaust film and the Rosenthal photograph taken after the flag raisers have raised the flag to a perpendicular position clearly indicate the individual in Position #6 is PFC Hayes (see Figure 5). [Encl (6)]
80. The del Valle report concluded that "The need for haste in identifying the participants (in order that they be present for the 7th War Loan Drive) precluded a more thorough investigation originally." This haste caused confusion as to the identity of the flag raisers. [Encl (2)]
81. PhM2c Bradley wrote to his parents on 26 February 1945, "I had a little to do with raising the American flag and it was the happiest moment of my life." [Ref (h), p. 216)]

Figure 6: Annotated photograph taken by PFC Campbell of the first flag as the second flag is being readied behind and out of the picture with PhM2c Bradley in the foreground.
Sgt Genaust and Mr. Rosenthal are the two individuals posing to the left of the flag pole.

82. PhM2c Bradley wrote to MajGen del Valle on 26 December 1946, "Things happened so fast I didn't think much of this flag raising until we returned to the U.S. from Iwo Jima." [Encl (2)]

Opinions

a. Previous attempts to accurately identify the flag raisers in Mr. Rosenthal's iconic photograph were complicated by the death of key participants, the stress of combat, the lack of recognition as to the significance of the second flag raising at the time of its occurrence, the haste to include the flag raisers in the 7th War Loan Drive, and the subsequent passage of time. [FF 29, 80, 82]

b. The April 1945 effort to comply with the directive to immediately return the flag raisers in Mr. Rosenthal's iconic photograph and have them participate in the 7th War Loan Drive resulted in Marine Corps officials incorrectly identifying some of the second flag raisers. [FF 80]

c. PhM2c Bradley, PFC Hayes, and PFC Gagnon may have felt pressured to maintain PFC Gagnon's original identification of the flag raisers in support of the 7th War Loan Drive. [FF 80]

d. The traumatic injuries PhM2c Bradley sustained in combat on 12 March 1945 may have resulted in him not thinking further about the flag raising or his role in it until after his return to the United States. [FF 29]

e. PhM2c Bradley may have conflated his participation in the first flag raising with the second flag raising. [FF 29, 81, 82]

f. The individual in Position #1 is Cpl Harlon Block. [FF 1, 16, 34, 35]

g. The individual in Position #2 is PFC Rene Gagnon. [FF 4, 16, 31, 44, 45, 46, 47]

h. The individual in Position #3 is not PhM2c John Bradley. [FF 50, 52, 53, 54, 55]

i. The individual in Position #3 is PFC Franklin R. Sousley. [FF 1, 16, 32, 50, 51, 53, 54, 55]

j. The individual in Position #4 is not PhM2c Bradley. [FF 56, 58, 59, 61, 63, 65]

k. The individual associated with Position #4 in the Genaust film is Sgt Strank. [FF 1, 16, 32, 57, 58, 60, 61, 62, 63, 66]

l. During the first break in the Genaust film, Sgt Strank placed a helmet on top of the soft cover on his head. [FF 63, 64, 66]

m. The individual in Position #4 is Sgt Strank. [FF 1, 16, 32, 56, 57, 58, 60, 61, 62, 63, 64, 66]

n. The individual in Position #5 is not PFC Franklin Sousley. [FF 50, 51, 53, 54, 55]

o. The individual in Position #5 is PFC Harold Schultz. [FF 2, 13, 32, 33, 68, 69, 70, 71, 72, 73, 74, 75]

p. The Board has no opinion as to why PFC Schultz never identified himself as a flag raiser.

q. The individual in Position #6 is PFC Ira Hayes. [FF 1, 16, 32, 77, 78, 79]

r. PhM2c Bradley participated in the first flag raising and remained atop Mount Suribachi throughout the second flag raising. [FF 8, 9, 12, 32, 11011981]

s. The opinion of the Board is that the identification of the second flag raisers is as depicted in Figure 7. [FF 1–82]

Recommendations

1. That the records of Headquarters U.S. Marine Corps reflect the identification of the individuals in the photograph as follows:

    a. Position #1 Cpl Harlon Block
    b. Position #2 PFC Rene Gagnon
    c. Position #3 PFC Franklin Sousley
    d. Position #4 Sgt Michael Strank
    e. Position #5 PFC Harold Schultz
    f. Position #6 PFC Ira Hayes

2. That the Commandant of the Marine Corps should inform the Secretary of the Navy, Chief of Naval Operations, and Medical Officer of the Marine Corps of the results of this Board before they are made public.

3. That the Commandant of the Marine Corps should inform the appropriate relatives of Cpl Harlon Block, PFC Rene Gagnon, PFC Franklin Sousley, Sgt Michael Strank, PFC Harold Schultz, PFC Ira Hayes, and PhM2c John Bradley of the results of this Board before they are made public.

4. That the Commandant of the Marine Corps should issue a public statement regarding the correct identification of the second flag raisers. This statement should include acknowledgement of the collective efforts of all who contributed to telling the story of the sacrifices and heroic achievements of all Marines, Sailors, and Coast Guardsmen during the battle of Iwo Jima.

Figure 7: The Huly Board Determination of the Identities of the Six Flag Raisers in Mr. Rosenthal's Photograph

5. That the Commandant of the Marine Corps recognize that all previous efforts at identification were conducted in good faith and that no official blame be assessed for previous inaccuracies in the historical record.

6. That the Commandant of the Marine Corps direct that this Board report and associated records be deposited in the Marine Corps History Division's archives.

7. That the Office of Legislative Affairs should inform appropriate Members of Congress and congressional staff of the results of this Board before they are made public.

8. That Headquarters U.S. Marine Corps should make public the findings of this Board.

9. That the Commandant of the Marine Corps should coordinate the public release of the findings of this Board with the Office of U.S. Marine Corps Communication.

10. That the National Museum of the Marine Corps and other Marine Corps monuments, displays, and educational programs should be updated to reflect the correct identification of the second flag raisers.

APPENDIX C

Identification of Personnel in Flag Raising Photograph

Headquarters U.S. Marine Corps
Washington
Public Relations Section
Fleet Post Office
San Francisco, California

19 April 1945

From: The Public Relations Officers

To: The Director, Division of Public Relations, Headquarters, U.S. Marine Corps.

Subject: Identification of personnel in flag raising photograph.

Reference: (a) Ltr AG-467-eig, 2065-85, 20 March 1945.

(1) The following is an identification and status of the flag raisers on Mount Suribachi who were shown in the enlargement of a square from a 16 mm. motion picture sequence photographed by Marine Sergeant William Genaust.

(2) Reading from left to right, they are: (1) Private First Class Franklin R. Sousley, 20 (942297), of Ewing, Kentucky, killed in action. (2) Sergeant Michael Strank, 26, (275228), of 121 Pine Street, Conemaugh, Pennsylvania, killed in action. (3) Private First Class Ira Hamilton Hayes, 22, (448804), of Bapchule, Arizona, Indian Agency, Gila River. The hands of this man on far side of pole are about all that shows of him clearly. He is effective, and returned to the USA, (4) Private First Class René A. Gagnon, 20, (808276), of 43 Hollis Street, Manchester, New Hampshire, effective and returned to the USA, (5) Pharmacist Mate

Second Class John Henry Bradley, USNR, (8681881), of 1112 West 8th Somerville, Massachusetts, killed in action.

3. The above information was furnished by the Commanding Officer of "E" Company, Second ` Battalion, 28th Marines, Fifth Marine Division. All men were members of that outfit.

Robert L. Jones

Notes

Prologue

1 George Greeley Wells, USMC Oral History Interview, November 6, 2008. Col Dave E. Severance, USMC Oral History Interview, November 7, 2008.
2 Ibid.
3 Ibid.

Chapter 1: Before

1 W. F. Craven and J. L. Cate (eds), *The Army Air Forces in World War II*: Vol. V., *The Pacific—Matterhorn to Nagasaki (June 1944 to August 1945)*. Chicago: University of Chicago Press, 1953. Eric Hammel, *Air War Pacific: Chronology, America's Air War Against Japan in East Asia and the Pacific, 1941–1945*. Pacifica, Calif.: Pacifica Press, 1998.
2 Eric Hammel, *Iwo Jima: Portrait of a Battle*. St. Paul, Minn.: Zenith Press, 2006.
3 Robert Sherrod, *History of Marine Corps Aviation in World War II*. San Rafael, Calif.: Presidio Press, 1980.
4 Eric Hammel, *Pacific Warriors: The U.S. Marines in World War II, A Pictorial Tribute*. St. Paul, Minn.: Zenith Press, 2005.
5 George W. Garand and Truman R. Strobridge, *Western Pacific Operations*. Vol. IV, *History of U.S. Marine Corps Operations in World War II*. Washington, D.C.: United States Marine Corps, 1971.
6 Ibid.
7 Ibid.
8 Ibid.

Chapter 2: Invasion

1 Fred Haynes and James A. Warren, *The Lions of Iwo Jima*. New York: Henry Holt and Company, 2008.
2 www.bayonetstrength.150m.com "The United States Marine Battalion, mid 1944 to mid 1945."
3 National World War II Museum. The Digital Collections: David Severance. Col Dave E. Severance, USMC Oral History Interview, November 7, 2008.
4 Ibid.
5 Ibid.
6 "Lieutenant Colonel Chandler W. Johnson is Awarded Legion of Merit." *Evanston (Illinois)*

Review, October 28, 1943.

7 Richard Wheeler, *The Bloody Battle for Suribachi.* New York, Skyhorse Publishing, 2007.

8 Severance, Colonel Dave E. USMC Oral History Interview, November 7, 2008.

9 Wikipedia biography of John Bradley.

10 James Bradley with Ron Powers, *Flags of Our Fathers.* New York, Bantam Books, 2000. Wheeler.

11 Ibid.

12 Bradley and Powers.

13 Ibid.

14 Ibid.

15 Severance oral history interview.

16 Wheeler.

17 Ibid.

18 Ibid.

19 George W. Garand and Truman R. Strobridge, *Western Pacific Operations.* Vol. IV, *History of U.S. Marine Corps Operations in World War II.* Washington, D.C.: United States Marine Corps, 1971. LtCol Whitman S. Bartley *Iwo Jima: Amphibious Epic.* Washington, D.C.: Marine Corps Historical Branch, 1954.

20 Wikipedia biography of Donald J. Ruhl.

21 Wikipedia biography of John Keith Wells.

22 Wheeler.

23 Ruhl Wikipedia biography.

24 Wheeler

25 Garand and Strobridge. Haynes and Warren.

26 Joe Rosenthal and W. C. Heinz, "The Picture That Will Live Forever," *Collier's Weekly,* February 18, 1955.

27 Encyclopedia Britannica. www.britannica.com/biography/Edward-Willis-Scripps#ref162161

28 Wikipedia biography of Joe Rosenthal. Rosenthal and Heinz.

29 Ibid.

30 Ibid.

31 Bradley and Powers.

32 Garand and Strobridge.

33 Bradley and Powers.

Chapter 3: Operation Hot Rocks

1 George W. Garand and Truman R. Strobridge, *Western Pacific Operations.* Vol. IV, *History of U.S. Marine Corps Operations in World War II.* Washington, D.C.: United States Marine Corps, 1971. LtCol Whitman S. Bartley, *Iwo Jima: Amphibious Epic.* Washington, D.C.: Marine Corps Historical Branch, 1954.

2 Fred Haynes and James A. Warren, *The Lions of Iwo Jima.* New York: Henry Holt and Company, 2008.

3 Bartley.

4 James Bradley with Ron Powers, *Flags of Our Fathers.* New York, Bantam Books, 2000.

5 Haynes and Warren.

6 Bradley and Powers.

7 Ibid.

8 "His men" refers to four volunteers from Pennell's 2nd Platoon, Company E: Squad leader

Sgt Michael Strank and all three members of one of Strank's fire teams: Cpl Harlon Block, PFC Ira Hayes, and PFC Franklin Sousley.

9   Bradley and Powers
10 Garand and Strobridge.
11 Bradley and Powers.
12 Bartley. Bradley and Powers.
13 Bradley and Powers.
14 Richard Wheeler, *The Bloody Battle for Suribachi.* New York, Skyhorse Publishing, 2007. Bradley and Powers.
15 Wheeler.
16 Bradley and Powers.
17 Ibid.
18 Ibid.
19 Ibid.
20 Wikipedia biography of Ernest Ivy Thomas, Jr.
21 Bartley.
22 Ibid.
23 Ibid.
24 Garand and Strobridge.
25 Bartley.
26 Haynes and Warren.
27 Action Report: Landing Team 328, Iwo Jima Operation.
28 Action Report: Landing Team 228, Iwo Jima Operation.
29 Garand and Strobridge.

Chapter 4: The First Flag

1   Letter from Ira Hayes to Mrs. Ada Belle Block, July 12, 1946. Compliments of *Leatherneck.*
2   George W. Garand and Truman R. Strobridge, *Western Pacific Operations.* Vol. IV, *History of U.S. Marine Corps Operations in World War II.* Washington, D.C.: United States Marine Corps, 1971. Lt-Col Whitman S. Bartley *Iwo Jima: Amphibious Epic.* Washington, D.C.: Marine Corps Historical Branch, 1954.
3   Ibid.
4   James Bradley with Ron Powers, *Flags of Our Fathers.* New York, Bantam Books, 2000.
5   Ibid.
6   Col Dave E. Severance, USMC Oral History Interview, November 7, 2008.
7   Wikipedia biography of Harold George Schrier.
8   Wikipedia, "Raising the Flag on Iwo Jima."
9   "Raising the Flag on Iwo Jima."
10 Severance oral history interview.
11 Raymond Jacobs, "Iwo Jima, February 23, 1945: First Flag Raising, An Eyewitness Account by Radioman Raymond Jacobs."
12 Bradley and Powers.
13 Ibid.
14 Herb Richardson, "Iwo Jima," *Leatherneck,* February 1980.
15 U.S. Marine Corps Report of the Huly Board Review of Information Regarding the Identity of the First Flag Raisers Atop Mount Suribachi, Iwo Jima, July 5–8, 2016.

16 Jacobs.
17 Richardson. Fred Haynes and James A. Warren, *The Lions of Iwo Jima*. New York: Henry Holt and Company, 2008.
18 Naval History and Heritage Command Oral History. "Iwo Jima Flag Raising: Recollections of the Flag Raising On Mount Suribachi During the Battle of Iwo Jima." Pharmacist Mate Second Class John H. Bradley, USN, with the 5th Marine Division. Hereafter Bradley Oral History. This interview was conducted while Bradley was a patient at Bethesda National Naval Medical Center in late April 1945.
19 Ibid.
20 Charles W. Lindberg, USMC Oral History Interview, October 18, 1985.
21 Severance oral history interview.
22 Jacobs.
23 Ibid.
24 Wikipedia biography of Henry Oliver Hansen.
25 Wikipedia article, "Marine Raiders."
26 Wikipedia biography of Charles W. Lindberg. World War II History Roundtable Oral History Night, Volume 5-5, February 13, 1992, by Charles W. Lindberg.
27 Tom Bartlett, obituary for Louis R. Lowery, 1916–1987, *Leatherneck*.
28 Ibid.
29 Identities derived from a photograph taken by SSgt Louis Lowery shortly after the first flag was raised. "Raising the Flag on Iwo Jima."
30 Jacobs.
31 Lindberg oral history interview.
32 Jacobs.
33 "Raising the Flag on Iwo Jima."
34 Jacobs.
35 Ibid.
36 Lindberg oral history interview.
37 Jacobs.
38 Ibid.
39 Ibid.

Chapter 5: The Second Flag

1 Col Mary H. Reinwald, "Confirming the First Flag Raisers: The Huly Panel Reconvenes." *Leatherneck:* October 2016.
2 Reinwald.
3 Karal Ann Marling and John Wetenhall, *Iwo Jima: Monuments, Memories, and the American Hero.* Cambridge, Massachusetts: Harvard University Press, 1991.
4 Wikipedia biography of Joe Rosenthal.
5 Wikipedia biography of Bill Genaust.
6 Ibid.
7 Norman T. Hatch, "Flags Over Mount Suribachi," *Marine Corps Gazette,* February 2004.
8 Wikipedia, "Raising the Flag on Iwo Jima."
9 Letter from Ira Hayes to Ada Belle Block, July 12, 1946.
10 "Raising the Flag on Iwo Jima."
11 Wikipedia biography of René Gagnon.

12   Fred Haynes and James A. Warren, *The Lions of Iwo Jima*. New York: Henry Holt and Company, 2008.
13   Wikipedia biography of Michael Strank.
14   Wikipedia biography of Franklin Sousley.
15   Wikipedia biography of Ira Hayes.
16   Marling and Wetenhall. "Raising the Flag on Iwo Jima."
17   Rosenthal Wikipedia biography.
18   Hayes to Block.
19   The Pulitzer Prizes, "Joe Rosenthal and the Flag-Raising On Iwo Jima." *www.pulitzer.org/article/joe-rosenthal-and-flag-raising-iwo-jima*
20   Hayes to Block
21   Thomas Patterson, *Best of America: The Inside Story of the Famous Iwo Jima Photo.* CNN, February 23, 2016.
22   Sousley Wikipedia biography.
23   "Raising the Flag on Iwo Jima."
24   The Unsung Filmmaker of Iwo Jima. www.jcs-group.com/military/marine/iwo.html
25   Dave E. Severance, "Grappling with Mount Suribachi, Iwo Jima." *Leatherneck*, February 2004.
26   Hayes to Block.
27   Joe Rosenthal and W. C. Heinz, "The Picture That Will Live Forever," *Collier's*, February 18, 1955.
28   Rosenthal Wikipedia biography.
29   The Unsung Filmmaker of Iwo Jima.
30   Peter C. Chen, World War II Database: "Battle of Iwo Jima," 19 Feb 1945–26 Mar 1945.
31   Hayes to Block.
32   Rosenthal Wikipedia biography.
33   Marling and Wetenhall.
34   Hayes to Block.
35   The Pulitzer Prizes.

Chapter 6: Cropping History

1   Wikipedia, "Raising the Flag on Iwo Jima."
2   Ibid.
3   Karal Ann Marling and John Wetenhall, *Iwo Jima: Monuments, Memories, and the American Hero.* Cambridge, Massachusetts: Harvard University Press, 1991.
4   Ibid.
5   Ibid.
6   Ibid.
7   Wikipedia biography of Ernest I. Thomas, Jr.
8   Marling and Wetenhall.
9   Keyes Beech, "Hottest Flag Raising." *Leatherneck*, May 1945.
10   Patrick Brion, *Combat Camera: Norman T. Hatch.*
11   Dave E. Severance, "Grappling with Mount Suribachi, Iwo Jima." *Leatherneck*, February 2004.
12   The author met Joe Rosenthal in the mid-1980s at Marine Corps Combat Correspondents' Association meetings and had several casual, unrecorded conversations with him, at least one

touching on the second flag-raising. Rosenthal's candor with respect to how he felt about The Photo before he ever saw it was refreshing, captivating, and memorable.

13 "Raising the Flag on Iwo Jima."
14 Fred Haynes and James A. Warren, *The Lions of Iwo Jima.* New York: Henry Holt and Company, 2008.
15 Thomas Patterson, *Best of America: The Inside Story of the Famous Iwo Jima Photo.* CNN, February 23, 2016. Rosenthal Wikipedia biography.
16 Wikipedia biography of Robert Sherrod.

Chapter 7: Grinding Forward

1 Bill D. Ross, *Iwo Jima: Legacy of Valor.* New York: Vanguard Press, 1985. Lindberg oral history interview.
2 Richard F. Newcomb, *Iwo Jima.* New York: Holt, Rinehart & Winston, 1965.
3 Strank Wikipedia biography.
4 Wikipedia biography of Harlon Block.
5 Ross.
6 Wikipedia biography of Henry Hansen.
7 Franklin D. Roosevelt, "Address to Congress on the Yalta Conference," March 1, 1945.
8 U.S. Marine Corps Report of the Huly Board Review of Information Regarding the Identity of the First Flag Raisers Atop Mount Suribachi, Iwo Jima, July 5–8, 2016.
9 Ibid.
10 World War II Graves. www2graves.com/people/charlo-louis-charles/. Together We Served. https://marines.togetherweserved.com. Lance Bacon, "Marines Say Men In First Iwo Jima Flag-raising Photo Were Also Misidentified. *Marine Times,* August 24, 2016.
11 Thomas Wikipedia biography. James Bradley with Ron Powers, *Flags of Our Fathers.* New York, Bantam Books, 2000.
12 Newcomb.
13 The Unsung Filmmaker of Iwo Jima. www.jcs-group.com/military/marine/iwo.html
14 Genaust Wikipedia biography.
15 Ibid.
16 Mary R. Williams *Chronology: 1941–1945, U.S. Army in World War II.* Washington, D.C.: Center of Military History, 1984.
17 Ibid.
18 Bradley oral history interview.
19 Bradley and Powers.
20 Ibid.
21 Ibid.
22 Gagnon Wikipedia biography.
23 Bradley Wikipedia biography.
24 Both flags are in the possession and care of the National Museum of the Marine Corps in Triangle, Virginia. The first flag is rarely displayed but the larger second flag is, as of this writing, almost always on display.
25 Williams.
26 Ibid.
27 Bradley and Powers.
28 Sousley Wikipedia biography.
29 Williams.

Chapter 8: After

1   Patrick Brion, *Combat Camera: Norman T. Hatch.*
2   Ibid. The author interviewed Maj Norman T. Hatch about his Tarawa experiences at Hatch's home in 1969 and enjoyed a warm relationship until Hatch's death in 2017. A tape of the 1969 interview was donated by the author to the Marine Corps University Archives and the subjects covered in this section of this book were gleaned from at least a dozen unrecorded phone conversations over many years.
3   Hatch, Norman T. "Flags Over Mount Suribachi." *Marine Corps Gazette,* February 2004.
4   Ibid.
5   Ibid.
6   Paul Farhi, "The Iwo Jima Photo and the Man Who Helped Save it." *The Washington Post,* February 21, 2013.
7   Brion. Maj Norman Hatch passed away on April 22, 2017, at age 94.
8   Christopher Reed, Felix de Weldon obituary. *The Guardian,* June 19, 2003.
9   Wikipedia biography of Felix de Weldon. University of Missouri Truman Library Oral History Interview with Felix de Weldon, January 22, 1969.
10 University of Missouri Truman Library Oral History Interview with Felix de Weldon, January 22, 1969.
11 Ibid.
12 Wikipedia, "Raising the Flag on Iwo Jima."
13 De Weldon oral history interview.
14 "Raising the Flag on Iwo Jima."
15 Wikipedia, "Marine Corps War Memorial."
16 "Marine Corps War Memorial."
17 Military History Round Table DVD. Charles Lindberg, February 13, 1992.
18 "Marine Corps War Memorial."

Chapter 9: The Mighty 7th

1   Karal Ann Marling and John Wetenhall, *Iwo Jima: Monuments, Memories, and the American Hero.* Cambridge, Massachusetts: Harvard University Press, 1991.
2   Ibid.
3   Ibid.
4   Reinwald, Col Mary H. "Examining the Evidence: USMC Reviews Iwo Jima Flag Raising Photo." *Leatherneck,* August 2016.
5   James Bradley with Ron Powers, *Flags of Our Fathers.* New York, Bantam Books, 2000.
6   Action Report: Landing Team 228, Iwo Jima Operation.
7   Bradley and Powers.
8   Hayes Wikipedia biography.
9   Bradley and Powers.
10 Herb Richardson, "Iwo Jima," *Leatherneck,* February 1980.
11 Bradley and Powers.
12 Bradley Wikipedia biography.
13 Marling and Wetenhall.
14 Bradley oral history interview.
15 Ibid.
16 This is the official Marine Corps explanation for the flag swap. The popular alternative was

based on Chandler Johnson's desire to keep the first flag for preservation by the 2nd Battalion, 28th Marines. See chapter 5 for more-detailed explanations. See also Norman Hatch's February 2004 *Marine Corps Gazette* article, "Flags Over Mount Suribachi." Steadfastly reliable sources (chiefly Hatch for the official story versus Dave Severance) were still clashing over the accuracy of the two explanations as late as Hatch's death in 2017.

17 Bradley oral history interview
18 Bradley and Powers.
19 Hayes Wikipedia biography.
20 Marling and Wetenhall.
21 Bradley and Powers. Marling and Wetenhall.
22 Conner, Curator Owen L. "A Flag's Journey: The Story of the Iwo Jima Flag." National Museum of the Marine Corps.
23 Marling and Wetenhall.
24 Bradley and Powers.
25 Ibid.
26 Ibid. Marling and Wetenhall.
27 Marling and Wetenhall.
28 Bradley and Powers.
29 Marling and Wetenhall.
30 Ibid.
31 Ibid..
32 Ibid.
33 Joe Rosenthal and W. C. Heinz, "The Picture That Will Live Forever," *Collier's Weekly,* February 18, 1955.
34 Bradley and Powers.

Chapter 10: Block

1 Wikipedia, "Raising the Flag on Iwo Jima."
2 Block Wikipedia biography.
3 Hayes Wikipedia biography.
4 Letter from Ira Hayes to Ada Belle Block, July 12, 1946.
5 "Raising the Flag on Iwo Jima."
6 Block Wikipedia biography. John Bradley Wikipedia biography. Henry Oliver Hansen Wikipedia biography. Hayes Wikipedia biography.

Chapter 11: What Became of Them

1 Gagnon Wikipedia biography.
2 Joe Rosenthal and W. C. Heinz, "The Picture That Will Live Forever," *Collier's Weekly*, February 18, 1955.
3 As cited in Marling and Wetenhall: "Flag Hero Found Dead: Cold and Excess Alcohol Killed Indian of Iwo Fame." *New York Times*, January 25, 1955.
4 Raymond Jacobs, "Iwo Jima, February 23, 1945: First Flag Raising, An Eyewitness Account by Radioman Raymond Jacobs."
5 Jacobs Wikipedia biography.
6 Fred Haynes and James A. Warren, *The Lions of Iwo Jima*. New York: Henry Holt and Company, 2008.

7   Lindberg Wikipedia biography.
8   Lowery obituary.
9   Rosenthal Wikipedia biography.
10 Schrier Wikipedia biography.
11 Severance oral history interview.
12 U.S. Marine Corps Report of the Huly Board Review of Information Regarding the Identity of the First Flag Raisers Atop Mount Suribachi, Iwo Jima, July 5–8, 2016.
13 John Fiore, "Crawfordsville Says Goodbye to Iwo Jima Hero." www.leatherneck.com. James Bradley with Ron Powers, *Flags of Our Fathers*. New York, Bantam Books, 2000.
14 Reece Lodder, "Remembering Greeley: The Marine Who Carried the First Iwo Jima Flag," *Leatherneck*, April 2015.
15 Keith Wells Wikipedia biography.

Chapter 12: The Irishman and the Omahan

1   Matthew Hansen, "New Mystery Arises from Iconic Iwo Jima Image: History buff's analysis of the famous World War II photo challenges long-assumed truth." *Omaha World Herald*, November 23, 2014.
2   Ibid.
3   Olivia B. Waxman, "The Man Who's Really in That Iconic Iwo Jima Photo." *Time* magazine, June 24, 2016.
4   Harold Schultz Wikipedia biography.
5   Email exchange between Col Mary Reinwald, USMC (Ret.) and Eric Hammel.

Chapter 13: The Marines

1   Col Mary Reinwald email response to a query from the author. June 26, 2017.
2   Reinwald, "Examining the Evidence."
3   U.S. Marine Corps Report of the Huly Board Review of Information Regarding the Identity of the First Flag Raisers Atop Mount Suribachi, Iwo Jima, July 5–8, 2016.
4   Thomas Wikipedia biography.
5   Reinwald, "Examining the Evidence."
6   James Bradley with Ron Powers, *Flags of Our Fathers*. New York, Bantam Books, 2000.

Afterword

1   Col Mary H. Reinwald, "Examining the Evidence." *Leatherneck*, August 2016.

Bibliography

Bartley, Lieutenant Colonel Whitman S. *Iwo Jima: Amphibious Epic.* Washington, D.C.: Marine Corps Historical Branch, 1954.

Blakeney, Jane. *Heroes: U.S. Marine Corps, 1861–1955.* Blakeney Publishing, 1956.

Bradley, James, with Powers, Ron. *Flags of Our Fathers.* New York, Bantam Books, 2000.

Craven, W. F., and Cate, J. L. eds. *The Army Air Forces in World War II: Vol. V., The Pacific—Matterhorn to Nagasaki (June 1944 to August 1945).* Chicago: University of Chicago Press, 1953.

Garand, George W., and Strobridge, Truman R. *Western Pacific Operations.* Vol. IV, *History of U.S. Marine Corps Operations in World War II.* Washington, D.C.: United States Marine Corps, 1971.

Hammel, Eric. *Air War Pacific: Chronology, America's Air War Against Japan in East Asia and the Pacific, 1941–1945.* Pacifica, Calif.: Pacifica Press, 1998.

——. *Iwo Jima: Portrait of a Battle.* St. Paul, Minn.: Zenith Press, 2006.

——. *Pacific Warriors: The U.S. Marines in World War II, A Pictorial Tribute.* St. Paul, Minn.: Zenith Press, 2005.

Haynes, Fred, and Warren, James A. *The Lions of Iwo Jima.* New York: Henry Holt and Company, 2008.

Marling, Karal Ann, and Wetenhall, John. *Iwo Jima: Monuments, Memories, and the American Hero.* Cambridge, Massachusetts: Harvard University Press, 1991.

Nalty, Bernard C. and Crawford, Danny J. *The United States Marines on Iwo Jima: The Battle and the Flag Raisings.* Washington, D.C.: History and Museums Divison, Headquarters, U.S. Marine Corps, 1995.

Newcomb, Richard F. *Iwo Jima.* New York: Holt, Rinehart & Winston, 1965.

Ross, Bill D. *Iwo Jima: Legacy of Valor.* New York: Vanguard Press, 1985.

Sherrod, Robert. *History of Marine Corps Aviation in World War II.* San Rafael, Calif.: Presidio Press, 1980.

Toland, John. *The Rising Sun: The Decline and Fall of the Japanese Empire, 1936–1945.* New York: Random House, 1970.

Wheeler, Richard. *The Bloody Battle for Suribachi.* New York, Skyhorse Publishing, 2007.

Williams, Mary R. *Chronology: 1941–1945, U.S. Army in World War II.* Washington, D.C.: Center of Military History, 1984.

Index